A Framework
for Political Analysis

PRENTICE-HALL CONTEMPORARY POLITICAL THEORY SERIES

David Easton, *Editor*

DAVID EASTON

A Framework
for Political Analysis

PRENTICE-HALL, INC., ENGLEWOOD CLIFFS, N.J.

PRENTICE-HALL INTERNATIONAL, INC., *London*
PRENTICE-HALL OF AUSTRALIA, PTY., LTD., *Sydney*
PRENTICE-HALL OF CANADA, LTD., *Toronto*
PRENTICE-HALL OF INDIA (PRIVATE) LTD., *New Delhi*
PRENTICE-HALL OF JAPAN, INC., *Tokyo*

Chapter One is adapted, with permission, from my article "The Current Meaning of 'Behavioralism' in Political Science," which appeared in James C. Charlesworth (ed.), The Limits of Behavioralism in Political Science *(Philadelphia: The American Academy of Political and Social Science, October, 1962), pp. 1-25.*

Library of Congress Catalog Card Number: 65-12874

Printed in the United States of America

33018-C

Current printing (last digit):
12 11 10 9 8 7

*For
my mother
and
Mrs. J.*

Preface to
Contemporary Political Theory Series

This volume is part of a new series in political science that is devoted to empirically oriented theory. Nothing testifies more eloquently to the growing strength of empirical political theory than the conviction that now, after more than twenty-five hundred years of development, it is for the first time possible to think of building a publication series out of volumes devoted exclusively to the construction of such theory. The series is itself a sign of the times; we hope it will also provide a means for vigorously and creatively reinforcing the present tendencies.

This series will contribute to the development of contemporary political theory in several distinctive ways. First and foremost, our primary objective is to gather together brief but exciting monographs that will explore alternative approaches to empirical theory. Some of these may be concerned with general, overarching theories that seek to bring order and coherence to the whole field of political science. Others may devote themselves to less comprehensive, partial theories that help to integrate selected aspects of political life, intranational, international, and cross-national. Still others may seek to explore the theoretical assumptions of existing empirical research and to systematize and assess their findings in the hope of bringing added clarity to a subfield, enhancing its theoretical relevance, and giving it a new sense of purpose and direction. Although the main emphasis will be on stimulating the production of critical and creative works that deal with the substance of theories in such areas, on occasion it will be appropriate to include volumes that direct their attention to the methodological tasks of theory construction itself.

We expect the series to leave its impact on the development of theory in a second way. It will provide a single medium through which original monographs in empirical or descriptive theory can be assembled. We would hope thereby to stimulate and reinforce the broadest range of experimentation with respect to alternative approaches to theory. Underlying the whole series is the basic premise that only through innovative and courageous efforts in a multitude of divergent and conflicting directions will it be possible for a gradual and meaningful consensus to arise in the course of time with regard to the outlines of a useful general theory or set of partial theories. It is the very essence of the theoretical enterprise that, if and when it seems appropriate, it should feel free to sever itself from the bonds of traditional ways of looking at political life. By providing an established publishing outlet, we would hope to lend encouragement in this direction at a time when it is most needed.

Third, we would hope that the availability in a single series of a growing assemblage of volumes on empirical theory will have a decisive influence on teaching and training in this field. We are in a process of transition in political science toward a more rigorous science and the series may be seen as another small effort to aid the change.

With regard to teaching and training in the function, tasks, and substance of empirical theory, a strong desire to improve the facilities in political science has not been wanting. But a major barrier has blocked the way. We have lacked a sufficient number of serious monographs to provide enough scope and depth to make formal courses in this area feasible as well as desirable. We would expect that in due time this series would offer a core around which courses on empirical theory might be initially developed, or where they already exist, enriched. In themselves such courses would contribute immeasurably to attracting the best minds in each generation of students to the field of theory or in sensitizing them to the actual function of theory in empirical research. By testifying to the challenge that theory presents and to the opportunities for empirical research, the series should, in its long range effect, reinforce empirical theory as an appropriate and adventuresome area for teaching and research.

Preface

This book is the second in a projected tetralogy on empirically oriented political theory. *The Political System* was the first to appear and in it I argued the need to revise drastically our conceptions of the tasks of political theory. The dominance of historical and ethical theory had at that time virtually crushed out any small shoots of empirical theory that had reached the surface prior to World War II. Since the publication of that volume the same argument need no longer be pressed. Empirical theory has grown apace and promises an even more luxuriant growth for the future.

At the conclusion of *The Political System* I had half committed myself to a succeeding work on a substantive theory of political life and the present work is a partial fulfillment of the basic structure of ideas that I then had in mind. But I had thought that this task could be completed in two additional books; since then it has become apparent that at least three will be required.

The present and second work takes up where the last left off. It seeks to present what its title proclaims: a framework for the analysis of political systems. It sets out the form within which a substantive theory of political life can be cast. It is a form that can best be described as a systems analysis, but the phrase needs to be accepted with considerable caution. It has many shades of meaning and the one to be attributed to it here should be derived

ix

operationally; that is, it should be inferred exclusively from the text and not from the varied meanings given it by others in the whole area of the systems sciences.

In this book I have set out to develop a logically integrated set of categories, with strong empirical relevance, that will make possible the analysis of political life as a system of behavior. I begin by identifying and elaborating the assumptions underlying an interpretation of politics as a system of behavior. On these assumptions, I then proceed to build a structure of concepts. But the reader is to be alerted against looking for anything more than the barest indication of how these concepts might be applied in practice. Here I have set up the briefest of scaffoldings. In a third book that will succeed this one in short order, I propose to put these concepts to work. But from the present introduction it will quickly become apparent that what I am seeking is a way of unveiling the basic processes through which a political system, regardless of its generic or specific type, is able to persist as a system of behavior in a world either of stability or of change. I shall be probing what I shall call the life processes of political systems as such, not the processes unique to any given type of system, democratic, dictatorial, bureaucratic, traditional, imperial or otherwise.

What will also become apparent in due course is that my attention will focus largely on the processes in systems, not on the structural forms through which these processes are served. Our need to understand structures is vital; but they can be analyzed successfully, it appears to me, only after we have thoroughly and unambiguously laid out the kinds of functions characteristic of political systems. To do otherwise is to put the cart before a nonexistent horse. Hence it is to a fourth and final theoretical work that I shall postpone the task of exploring the kinds of categories that would be necessary to enable us to understand variations in structure.

A brief outline of the central concepts of the present volume appeared in "An Approach to the Analysis of Political Systems."* Two circumstances that followed on the appearance of this article have greatly encouraged me to continue along the line of thought there initially set forth. First, the article itself was soon reprinted in a number of collections of readings in political science and sociology and was reproduced for consumption abroad in *Americana* (1956-7) and in the Italian edition of *The Political System*. Second, I was gratified to see the extent to which, in a few brief years, scholars have found the ideas interesting enough to apply in their own empirical as well as theoretical research. In fact, because of this friendly reception at so early a stage in the development of my thinking, what I have to say in this book has lost some of the novelty it might otherwise have had.

* *World Politics* 9 (1957), 383-400.

But in compensation for whatever has been lost in this respect, I have a considerable amount of quite unexpected application and testing of concepts quite similar to those I have proposed, and on this material I shall be able to lean for illustrations both in this and especially in the next book.*

Since the publication of "An Approach to the Analysis of Political Systems" and other articles in which I have developed and applied parts of the same schema, some interest has arisen in the sources of this kind of approach. Roots of ideas are so delicately intertwined as often to defy accurate sorting and alignment so it is not strange that such comments as have appeared in print have on occasion been somewhat misleading.

Although the concept "system" is prominent in both sociology and economics, in particular, it would represent a profound misconstruction of these disciplines if we were to identify their theoretical perspectives with those that will be developed here. That there is overlap and development stands to reason; no one would wish to or could possibly ignore or neglect the contributions that both disciplines have made to our understanding of the operations of social systems. But the systems approach that I shall be elaborating draws its main inspiration from other sources. These can best be summed up as the systems sciences, at times more narrowly characterized as the communications sciences. They represent the products of the most recent theoretical revolution in systems conceptualization, one that goes far beyond the typical ways in which systems thinking has developed in sociology and economics. The mere fact that I shall be speaking of inputs and outputs, for example, ought not to be misconstrued for the adoption of the

---

* For some examples with respect to "demands" particularly, see M. Weiner, *The Politics of Scarcity* (Chicago: University of Chicago Press, 1962), especially chapter 9; T. Parsons, "General Theory in Sociology" in *Sociology Today*, R. K. Merton, L. Broom, and L. S. Cottrell, Jr., eds. (New York: Basic Books, Inc., 1959), pp. 3-38, especially p. 19; and also T. Parsons, "On the Concept of Political Power" *Proceedings of the American Philosophical Society* 107 (1963), 232-62, especially p. 234. For the technical use of "demands" together with other concepts such as "inputs," "outputs," and "conversion," and some form of systems model, see, among others, G. A. Almond, "A Functional Approach to Comparative Politics" in *The Politics of Developing Areas*, G. A. Almond and J. S. Coleman, eds. (Princeton: Princeton University Press, 1960), pp. 3-66, especially pp. 14-17; G. A. Almond and S. Verba, *The Civic Culture* (Princeton: Princeton University Press, 1963), especially p. 15; J. C. Wahlke, H. Eulau *et al.*, *The Legislative System* (New York: John Wiley & Sons, Inc., 1962), chapter 1; W. C. Mitchell, *The American Polity* (New York: The Free Press of Glencoe, Inc., 1962), especially Chapter 12. Not that others have always interpreted the concepts in precisely the same way as they appeared in the *World Politics* article of 1957. But they are sufficiently similar in interpretation to enable us to begin to think of at least a coalescence or convergence of basic theoretical perspectives. If this is so, we have indeed moved a long way from the condition in which our discipline found itself at the time *The Political System* was published in 1953.

input-output analysis familiar to students of economics. Any similarities, the reader will quickly discover, are indeed largely coincidental.

But as I cautioned earlier, the framework elaborated here has not been able to lean on any ready-made model; and no eclectic borrowing from other varying kinds of systems approaches would do. A consistent structure of concepts had to be newly developed that would fit the kind of system that political life constitutes.

Perhaps the institutional setting within which some of my formative thinking took place will help to clarify the reasons for associating my theoretical approach more closely with the systems sciences in general than with any single social or, for that matter, natural science in particular. Although I was already in the midst of experimenting with my own particular variant of systems analysis, one that I consider more closely attuned to the subject matter of politics, it was participation in an interdisciplinary group of extraordinary breadth at the University of Chicago, the Committee on Behavioral Sciences, that helped to hasten my appreciation of the valuable insights offered by the general approach of the systems sciences and that helped to enrich my understanding of it.

This committee was brought together in 1951, primarily under the initiative of James G. Miller, then chairman of the Department of Psychology at the University of Chicago, to devote itself to a prolonged and intensive discussion of common problems in a systems approach as viewed from all the sciences, physical, biological and social.* Through what we liked to think of as the wisdom and foresight of Ralph W. Tyler, then Dean of the Division of the Social Sciences and now Director of the Center for Advanced Study in the Behavioral Sciences, and of Dr. Lowell T. Coggeshall, then Dean of the Division of the Biological Sciences and now Vice-President and Trustee of the University of Chicago, we were able to obtain a suite of offices for our purposes. There we met for a full day every Tuesday, for about two years, with lunch served from our own kitchen on the premises. My association with a number of the core members of this Committee was continued for still another year when I commuted one day a week between Chicago and Ann Arbor to participate in the Theory Seminar of the Mental Health Research Institute at the University of Michigan, the inheritor of the original Committee.

* Our committee consisted of the following core members: Donald T. Campbell, psychology; Robert Crane, history; David Easton, political science; Donald W. Fiske, psychology; Ralph W. Gerard, neurophysiology; Dr. Henrietta Herbolsheimer, internal medicine; James G. Miller, psychology; Jacob Marschak, economics; Richard L. Meier, planning; John R. Platt, physics; Anatol Rapoport, mathematical biology; Roger Sperry, biology; Sherwood Washburn, anthropology. Around these floated a somewhat larger and changing group from all disciplines at the University, together with distinguished visitors invited from around the country.

In the Committee, after we had overcome some initial difficulties created by varying languages, perspectives, and expectations with regard to method—common concepts for dissimilar phenomena, different concepts for almost identical phenomena, varying emphases on the need for quantification first rather than en route—we were able to settle down to the discussion of what quickly became apparent to many of us: The perspectives of a systems analysis serve to link all of the sciences, natural and social, help to make communication among them possible and rewarding, and generate common kinds of problems that interdisciplinary discussion can help to resolve. The experience of this committee strongly reinforced my conviction of the plausibility and fruitfulness of continued work within the newer systems frame of reference.

On a more personal plane, I owe a special debt to John R. Platt of our Department of Physics for the many conversations we have had with regard to systems research and for the more occasional but stimulating discussions with Donald W. Fiske and John M. Butler of our Department of Psychology. I have also benefited from the opportunity for a continuing exchange of ideas with Leonard Binder of my own Department in our joint Seminar on Political Change, from chats with my former colleagues, Myron Weiner and David E. Apter, and from the enlightening discussions that the too infrequent crossing of our paths has permitted with Karl W. Deutsch, Heinz Eulau, Bertram M. Gross, George Modelski, and David J. Singer. In addition, Lawrence Senesh of Purdue University has in the last year helped in the clarification of some of my ideas through his conviction that basic concepts in the social sciences can be translated into simple enough language so as to be made accessible for systematic instruction at the very earliest grades in elementary school. This is a task that he has already demonstrated to be entirely feasible.

Since my ideas have been taking shape in courses and publications over a good number of years, numerous former graduate students, some of whom were my assistants, and all of whom now have their own teaching, research, or other responsibilities, have contributed to my thinking. They have done this in their own special ways by faithfully adhering to the scientific code of doubt, challenge, improvement, and reconstruction. Among them I would mention particularly Ellen Samuels Baar, Reginald Bartholomew, Peter Clark, Jack Dennis, Roger D. Masters, John D. McCaffrey, Tadao Okamura, and Aristide Zolberg.

Finally, for financial assistance and for permitting me the time to devote to specific aspects of the research, I wish to thank the Social Science Research Committee of the Division of the Social Sciences at the University of Chicago, and the Ford Foundation for making possible a Ford Research Professorship in Governmental Affairs, 1960-61. The benefits of a year as a fellow at the Center for Advanced Study in the Behavioral Sciences at Stanford, California, 1957-58, have been incalculable.

As usual, my wife has shared in the development of the ideas contained in this volume and in the editing and revision of each successive manuscript. Convention alone forbids expression of the true measure of her continuing and intensive intellectual involvement and contributions over the years.

DAVID EASTON

Table of Contents

ONE

Theory and Behavioral Research

This book is about a new kind of theoretical approach to the analysis of political life, one that for want of a more descriptive name may be called *systems analysis*. The selection of systems analysis as the major approach to political theory reflects only one of a number of possible significant strategies for the construction of general political theory.[1] But it is

1 For other approaches see: G. A. Almond, "A Functional Approach to Comparative Politics" in *The Politics of Developing Areas*, G. A. Almond and J. S. Coleman, eds. (Princeton: Princeton University Press, 1960), pp. 3-66; K. W. Deutsch, *The Nerves of Government* (New York: Free Press of Glencoe, Inc., 1963); S. N. Eisenstadt, *The Political Systems of Empires* (New York: Free Press of Glencoe, Inc., 1963); C. J. Friedrich, *Man and His Government* (New York: McGraw-Hill Book Company, 1963); H. D. Lasswell and A. Kaplan, *Power and Society* (New Haven: Yale University Press, 1950); H. D. Lasswell, *The Decision Process: Seven Categories of Functional Analysis* (College Park: University of Maryland, Bureau of Governmental Research, 1956); W. C. Mitchell, *The American Polity* (New York: Free Press of Glencoe, Inc., 1962); and various articles on politics by Talcott Parsons such as " 'Voting' and the Equilibrium of the American Political System" in *American Voting Behavior*, E. Burdick and A. J. Brodbeck, eds. (New York: Free Press of Glencoe, Inc., 1959), pp. 80-120; "On the Concept of Political Power," *Proceedings of the American Philosophical Society*, 107 (1963), 232-62; "On the Concept of Influence" *Public Opinion Quarterly*, 27 (1963), 37-92; "Some Highlights of the General Theory of Action" in *Approaches to the Study of Politics,*

one that permits us to take advantage of a conceptual revolution well under way not only in a host of neighboring disciplines, but in the biological and natural sciences as well.

It is always possible to borrow the conceptual apparatus of other disciplines and apply them analogically to the data of a different field. Even if a person were to attempt nothing more than this, it could prove extremely useful for the stimulation of theoretical research in politics. In the history of science, analogy and metaphor have more than once served as the source of new insights and fundamental transformations in thought. Political science has consistently shared in this use of models of analysis borrowed from other fields.[2]

In political theory today we are ready to go far beyond this. We can explore the basic outlines of a conceptual structure based upon the adoption and specific adaptation of systems analysis for the understanding of political life. In the process, as must be the case with any genuine effort to build on central concepts borrowed from some other fields and perspectives, theoretical research in systems terms takes on many new dimensions, and old concepts acquire new and often unrecognizable content. Although, in the outcome, systems analysis—as adapted for purposes of social research—remains within the same general conceptual terrain in which it has grown up, we shall find by the end of our examination of it that it has gone off in substantially different directions. Biological and natural scientists would no longer feel at home in it, although it might well stir faint and nostalgic memories of a conceptual homeland that they once knew.

In this volume I shall seek to sketch a map of the new terrain, showing its outer limits and the contours of the major formations. I shall be looking at the new conceptual structure through a weak telescope, as it were, so that we shall not be overwhelmed by the detail. In a succeeding volume I shall seek to bring a more powerful lens to bear upon a systems analysis of

---

R. Young, ed. (Evanston, Ill.: Northwestern University Press, 1958), pp. 282-304. For an interesting statement on the current problems of political theory, see J. G. March, "Some Observations on Political Theory" in *Politics and Public Affairs*, L. K. Caldwell, ed. (Bloomington: Indiana University, 1962), pp. 121-39.

2 See M. Landau, "On the Use of Metaphor in Political Analysis," *Social Research*, 28 (1961), 331-53, especially p. 353 where the author concludes that "Political science has always resorted to metaphors, to the device of proceeding from the known to the unknown. Those who criticize the use of 'models' need to understand that they too must use them. Accordingly, much of the conflict over the use of models is spurious. The choice is not between models and no models, but between a critical consciousness of their use and an uncritical acceptance. An open and 'hygienic' use of models may or may not aid us in developing empirically sound political theory, but it would enable us to run far less risk than we take with the hidden, implicit, and rigidified metaphors that one frequently finds in the textbooks of political science."

political life. After the present preliminary excursion, we shall be less likely to lose our way in the considerable theoretical detail that will then be available and necessary.

THE REVOLUTION IN POLITICAL THEORY

When my volume, *The Political System,*[3] was first published, there was a transparent need to argue the case for the construction of empirically oriented general theory in political science. It is an index of the gargantuan strides that have been made in the development of political science as a discipline that what was then an entirely appropriate subject for intense discussion, has now come to be taken for granted. Many might still challenge the capacity of the discipline to generate such useful general theories at the present stage of development in political science itself and in the social sciences as a whole. But only a diminishing and archaic few remain who would deny the utility of efforts in this direction. There are fewer still who would be wanton enough to undertake some empirical research without seeking to tie it, however modestly, into a broader theoretical context.

Indeed, the remarkable feature about this intellectual revolution has been the rate at which the whole discipline has been able to shift direction and yet remain in basic control of its intellectual apparatus. It stands as testimony to the rich reservoir of talent, skills, and inherited knowledge that have become embodied in political science as a discipline. In so short a time a revolution in general perspectives has occurred, new concepts are being proliferated at an ever increasing pace, and new conceptual structures, with varying degrees of explicitness, have been advanced for research and serious consideration.

All this has been taking place under the rubric of an intellectual upheaval that has been felt throughout the social sciences and that has for some time been identified as the behavioral approach. The new kind of theory in political science that has been struggling through a decade of parturition and that is just now beginning to take on a life of its own, is largely an offspring of this revolution. Its successful birth promises in turn, to give the behavioral approach new direction and inspiration. As a product of and in relation to this movement, empirically oriented political theory is often referred to as behavioral theory.

To appreciate the part that the new theorizing has begun to play in the orientations and progress of political science and to understand how inextricably it is mingled with the growth of political behavior as a distinctive

[3] D. Easton, *The Political System* (New York: Alfred A. Knopf, Inc., 1953).

approach in political research, it is important to explore the meaning of this great upheaval. What is meant by behavioral research with respect to political life? An answer to this question will reveal the central role that empirically oriented theory has begun to play in the transformation of political science as a discipline. It will put one particular approach to general theory, that of systems analysis, in a more general context.

BEHAVIORAL RESEARCH AS A MOVEMENT

Political behavior stands for both an intellectual tendency and a concrete academic movement. As a tendency, it is an intellectual current that may be found among many students of politics, in some minor degree at least; as a movement, it has many fewer outright adherents and advocates. So much is clear and, with respect to it, we could probably obtain agreement from those more or less associated with this point of view. But beyond this the approach is so new and its limits so poorly defined that it is doubtful whether we could arrive at a consensus on its positive aspects. First, we would find it extremely difficult to come to terms about who among political scientists ought to be identified as behavioral researchers—that is, about who are the authentic members of the movement or its valid practitioners. Second, we would also find sharp disagreement on where the emphasis in behavioral research ought to lie—that is, on its nature as an intellectual enterprise.

Let us consider the first point. The criteria for membership in the movement are as loose and ambiguous as the boundaries are vague and arguable. As in most social movements, membership is not a matter of belonging to a formal organization but one of possessing a sense of belonging together, sharing similar assumptions and ideals, respecting one another's interests, seeking reciprocal aid and sustenance, or accepting a common leadership.

There are, however, some physical symbols and behavior patterns that do distinguish the movement. Its adherents have tended to publish through a limited number of periodicals,[4] and, unexpectedly, the movement has even evoked a limited degree of specialization in the choice of book publishers. Although the movement has never crystallized in a formal sense, there are structures such as the Social Science Research Council's Committee on Political Behavior and its Committee on Comparative Politics that have provided some institutional focus in at least these two fields. Furthermore, some time ago, the feeling of the adherents was sufficiently strong to stimulate discussion about the advisability of establishing separate institu-

---

[4] Such as the *Public Opinion Quarterly, World Politics, American Behavioral Scientist,* and *Behavioral Science.*

tions, such as a special journal[5] or organization. Unlike the fields of psychology, psychiatry, and other sciences where splinter associations have emerged, a special subdivision of the American Political Science Association providing institutional expression for the new approach never did materialize. The Association has proved sufficiently flexible to adapt with the necessary speed to the changing character of the field.[6]

But these material symbols have provided too informal a connection with the behavioral approach, and they have been too fragmented and limited in scope to offer a major or satisfying central focus for the movement. As a result, the movement has remained quite rudimentary, unable to generate a true sense of orthodoxy or inviolable tenets. The political science profession has thereby been spared the trauma of institutional schisms. But unexpected costs have been incurred. "Card-carriers" in the behavioral movement are not easy to distinguish from fellow-travelers, tolerant sympathizers, occasional supporters, or ambivalent critics. A person may be seen by traditionalists as belonging to an opposing camp, and yet the latter group at the same time may disown him for diametrically opposite reasons.

Perhaps some of the ambiguity also stems from the nature of the commitment required of a behavioralist. The behavioralist is not automatically prohibited or incapacitated from continuing traditional research where it seems necessary and appropriate, as in the study of the relationship among institutions. The behavioral approach has shown its greatest strength in research on individuals, especially in a face-to-face relationship, or with respect to a type of aggregative behavior such as voting. Small groups and organizations in their internal structure and processes and certain aspects of well-defined communities represent the maximal scope for which there have been contrived research techniques entirely harmonious with the assumptions of behavioralism. The techniques become less reliable and their results less valid when applied to the interrelationships of institutions such as party systems and legislatures, or electoral systems and parties, or the effect of alternative types of institutional arrangements on recruitment to positions of leadership and authority.[7]

[5] I think that it is fair to state that it was in the atmosphere of these discussions that the *American Behavioral Scientist* (formerly *PROD*) was founded on the initiative and responsibility of Alfred de Grazia.

[6] This in itself has a history which it would be interesting to explore if we are to understand the way in which a discipline successfully copes with changes in its intellectual objectives and methods, an adaptation that cannot by any means be taken for granted. In this history the roles of Evron M. Kirkpatrick, Executive Director of the American Political Science Association, and of Pendleton Herring, President of the Social Science Research Council, would loom very large.

[7] See M. Sherif and B. L. Koslin, *Theoretical and Research Reports: The*

Criticism to the contrary notwithstanding, it is the rare student of political behavior who overcommits himself to the limits of research as defined by his rigorous techniques. In practice, we find most behavioralists prepared to use the best available technical resources, even if it means that the traditional approach alone is feasible. The behavioralist is, in effect, a product mix of the traditional and the behavioral, weighted on the side of the latter. But it is the particular mixture that frequently leads to difficulty in identifying those who are authentic behavioralists.

POLITICAL BEHAVIOR AS AN
INTELLECTUAL TENDENCY

If my first point is that political behavior has many of the qualities of an inchoate social movement, my second one is that, just because the movement is so ill defined, it is far more easily described by reference to its intellectual content than to its membership. Most students of politics, even those unwilling to accept classification as behavioralists, would probably agree about the general nature of behavioral assumptions and objectives, although strong differences might arise concerning the precise emphasis to be given to any one of these.

What is the nature of these assumptions and objectives, the intellectual foundation stones on which this movement has been constructed? No single way of characterizing them is satisfactory to everyone, but the following itemized list provides a reasonably accurate and exhaustive account of them.[8]

"Institutional" vs. "Behavioral" Controversy in Social Science with Special Reference to Political Science (Norman: Institute of Group Relations, University of Oklahoma, 1960). The authors of this work, looking at political research from the perspectives of social psychology, loudly applaud the insistence on the institutional approach that we find in political science.

[8] Most of the items can be distilled from what is said about the behavioral approach in the following sources: J. C. Charlesworth, The Limits of Behavioralism in Political Science (Philadelphia: American Academy of Political and Social Science, 1962); M. Cowling, The Nature and Limits of Political Science (New York: Cambridge University Press, 1962); B. Crick, The American Science of Politics, Its Origins and Conditions (London: Routledge & Kegan Paul Ltd., 1959); R. A. Dahl, "The Behavioral Approach," American Political Science Review, 55 (1961), 763-72; M. Duverger, Methodes de la Science Politique (Paris: Presses Universitaires de France, 1959); Easton, The Political System, and "Traditional and Behavioral Research in American Political Science," Administrative Science Quarterly, 2 (1957), 110-15; H. Eulau, The Behavioral Persuasion (Stanford, Calif.: Stanford University Press, 1963); C. S. Hyneman, The Study of Politics (Urbana: University of Illinois Press, 1959); H. D. Lasswell, The Future of Political Science (New York: Atherton Press, 1963); W. G. Runciman, Social Science and Political Theory (New York: Cambridge University Press, 1963); D. B. Truman, "The Impact on Political Science of the

1. *Regularities.* There are discoverable uniformities in political behavior. These can be expressed in generalizations or theories with explanatory and predictive value.
2. *Verification.* The validity of such generalizations must be testable, in principle, by reference to relevant behavior.
3. *Techniques.* Means for acquiring and interpreting data cannot be taken for granted. They are problematic and need to be examined self-consciously, refined, and validated so that rigorous means can be found for observing, recording, and analyzing behavior.
4. *Quantification.* Precision in the recording of data and the statement of findings requires measurement and quantification, not for their own sake, but only where possible, relevant, and meaningful in the light of other objectives.
5. *Values.* Ethical evaluation and empirical explanation involve two different kinds of propositions that, for the sake of clarity, should be kept analytically distinct. However, a student of political behavior is not prohibited from asserting propositions of either kind separately or in combination as long as he does not mistake one for the other.
6. *Systematization.* Research ought to be systematic, that is, theory and research are to be seen as closely intertwined parts of a coherent and orderly body of knowledge. Research untutored by theory may prove trivial, and theory unsupportable by data, futile.
7. *Pure science.* The application of knowledge is as much a part of the scientific enterprise as theoretical understanding. But the understanding and explanation of political behavior logically precede and provide the basis for efforts to utilize political knowledge in the solution of urgent practical problems of society.
8. *Integration.* Because the social sciences deal with the whole human situation, political research can ignore the findings of other disciplines only at the peril of weakening the validity and undermining the generality of its own results. Recognition of this interrelationship will help to bring political science back to its status of earlier centuries and return it to the main fold of the social sciences.

This list probably includes all the major tenets of the behavioral credo

---

Revolution in the Behavioral Sciences," in *Research Frontiers in Politics and Government* (Washington, D.C.: The Brookings Institution, 1955), pp. 202-32, and "The Implications of Political Behavioral Research," *Items*, 5 (1951), 37-39; V. Van Dyke, *Political Science, A Philosophical Analysis* (Stanford, Calif.: Stanford University Press, 1960); D. Waldo, *Political Science in the United States of America* (Paris: UNESCO, 1956); *A Report of the Behavioral Sciences at the University of Chicago* (University of Chicago: Self-Study Committee, 1954); Editorial, "What is Political Behavior," *PROD*, 1 (1958), 42-43.

and represents the major differences between the behavioral and traditional modes of research. As such, we have a purely formal statement of the meaning of behavioralism, one that helps us less in understanding its meaning than in appreciating the nature of the kind of questions we must begin to ask. For, even if we were to have little difficulty in obtaining formal agreement to this list, there can be no doubt that major differences would immediately rise to the surface, not necessarily about the composition of the behavioral credo itself, but about the relative prominence of one or another of the articles.

As we review the varied explanations offered by behavioralists themselves, we find that, within the broad limits set by the credo, the behavioral approach has come to mean about as many things as there are commentators. Every man puts in his own emphasis and thereby becomes his own behavioralist. Does the approach exclusively employ the scientific method or is it just a mood favoring that method?[9] Does it represent the use of kinds of data hitherto absent from political research, especially the findings from such "hard-core" sciences as psychology, sociology, and anthropology,[10] or does it stand largely for a return to the individual as the focal point for political research?[11] May we interpret behavioralism even more broadly and flexibly and view it as a virtually empty bottle into which one pours any kind of wine, new or old, as long, presumably, as it is aromatic of science?[12] Whatever our point of view, we have authorities to whom we can turn to press out interpretation.

But complete interpretive anomie does not exist. Even though the relative emphases bring different aspects of the landscape into prominence and, momentarily, may even leave the impression that the authorities are geographically far apart, closer inspection does reveal that they are all looking ahead toward the same region in space—a science of politics modeled after the methodological assumptions of the natural sciences.

As I have suggested, this conclusion leaves us with a fundamental question still unanswered. If this is all that the revolt against tradition has really meant, if all that behavioralists are arguing for is the introduction of scientific method and nothing more, why are we not content with calling a spade a spade? Why has it been necessary or useful to mint and distribute a new conceptual currency—political behavior? After all, science is still an honored ideal in the United States. Indeed, during the 1920's and 1930's the

9 Dahl, "The Behavioral Approach."
10 Truman, "The Impact on Political Science."
11 Easton, *The Political System.*
12 "What is Political Behavior," *PROD.*

phrase "science of politics" was the preferred way for referring to the newer tendencies of the period out of which the modern revolt grew. Need we call the rose by any other name?

If we were satisfied to accept the explanation of political behavior as just the continued application of scientific method to politics begun in the 1920's and 1930's, we could quickly brush aside this change in terminology by attributing it to caprice, to the inexplicable alternations brought about by the fads of language, or to the need for a distinctive symbol of self-identification in the battles with established orthodoxy. Undoubtedly, such factors as these have a part in the diffusion of the behavioral label. However, if we stopped here and concluded that this is all that the new name conveys, we would be neglecting some essential substantive implications of a kind that show our discipline to be an integral part of a deeper shift taking place in the social sciences as a whole in our age. To appreciate the full and rich meaning of the behavioral trend in political research, we must broaden our horizons momentarily. We must pause to see this development as a reaction to and reflection of the fact that all the social sciences are together advancing to a new stage, one of increased scientific maturity, I am tempted to say, and one characterized by new theoretical aspirations.

THE INADEQUACY OF A
METHODOLOGICAL EXPLANATION

If we are content to accept the behavioral approach as just another way of signifying that its adherents are proposing to use the most advanced methods of social science and nothing more, we saddle ourselves with the following real problem. A number of other social sciences, such as the so-called hard-core sciences already mentioned, have for many years, well before World War II, looked upon themselves as devotees of the scientific method. Much of their labor has gone into clarifying and elaborating the methodological premises of the social sciences and developing sophisticated and rigorous techniques for accumulating, interpreting, and analyzing data. The striking point here is that, even though these disciplines so conceived of themselves in the interval between the wars, it is only since the 1950's that they too have come to describe themselves and to be designated by others as behavioral sciences.

As in the case of political science itself, we might argue that there is really nothing in a name, that the oscillation in nomenclature between social sciences and behavioral sciences is inconsequential and irrelevant. But, if ordinary common sense tells us little else, it does sensitize us to the fact that names do reflect and, often in anticipation, reinforce changes already taking place in the objects to which they refer. It is my argument that the name changes have precisely this meaning in the social sciences.

The inclusion of the study of political life as part of the behavioral sciences similarly hints that, regardless for the moment of the nature of the transformation that has taken place, it must involve more than just the importation into political science of the scientific method. It is for this reason that we cannot hope to understand the full connotations of the term "political behavior" unless we view it as part of the evolution of the social disciplines as a whole. It is just too deceptively easy to interpret it either as a synonym for what is virtuous in research or for scientific method; it is only partly correct to see in it an ideological weapon lending color and vigor to the movement of a diffuse and informal group of academic rebels against traditions.

Furthermore, it sells this new movement quite short. Such simplistic interpretations inadvertently lend credence to the very point that the most impassioned critics of political behavior have advanced. These critics have accused students of political behavior of selecting their problems not in the light of theoretical or ethical relevance, but largely on grounds of the accidental availability of technically adequate means for research. If a reliable technique is not at hand, the subject is not considered researchable. As a result of the admittedly early stages in the development of technical means of social research, the argument runs, the behavioral approach is able to deliver reliable knowledge only with regard to political commonplaces or trivia. The really significant problems of political life cannot be challenged by these means, the argument continues; hence, insistence upon the priority of technical competence manages to squeeze out the free play of insight and imagination.

This is neither the time nor place at which the merits of this criticism need to be weighed. But, from the viewpoint of the meaning of political behavior, if we were to concede that it merely conveys the tried and true phrase "scientific method," we could not help but leave the impression that its critics were not too far wrong. It would represent basically a change in mood in favor of scientific methodology, methods, and techniques, with the emphasis on the latter.

No one could argue that it does not represent these things, and if it did nothing else, it would be a significant enough contribution. We cannot stop at this point, however, if we seek to do full justice to this tendency. It would lead us to neglect or ignore entirely an equally crucial contribution of a substantive kind, one that helps to build a major bridge between political science and its neighboring disciplines on the one side and the future of political research on the other.

HISTORICAL PERSPECTIVE

The past

To appreciate how far the emergence of a behavioral approach goes beyond a methodological or merely technical reorientation, we have to put recent trends in political research into the context of the whole historical movement of the social sciences. The quickest way of doing this, without becoming enmeshed in the intricacies of their history, is to trace the evolution in names used to identify what we are coming to call the behavioral sciences. These names mirror the essence of the historical transformations relevant to our immediate purposes.

Historically, all social knowledge was originally one and indivisible; the intellectual specialization of labor appears late upon the scholarly scene in the Western world. For almost two thousand years, from the early classical Greek period to sometime in the eighteenth century, men basically saw each other not as specialists but as general seekers after wisdom and knowledge, as philosophers in the original sense of the word. It is true, as early as the Middle Ages, that law, theology, and medicine stood as separate and coordinate fields of learning and teaching in the universities; but philosophy still embraced the bulk of human knowledge about man in society.

With the increasing weight and differential rate and direction of the development of knowledge in the modern historical periods, however, this general corpus gradually began to break up into specialized segments. By the eighteenth century, for example, we can already distinguish what came to be called natural philosophy from moral philosophy, and, as knowledge in both these fields increased remarkably during that century, their names underwent a further subtle modification. Under the heightening prestige of chemistry, physics, and biology, they acquired the names natural and moral sciences. With further elaboration during the nineteenth century, especially under the impetus of Saint-Simon and Auguste Comte, with their sharp focus on human relationships in society, the moral sciences finally became known by the contemporary phrase, social sciences. Of course, ethical inquiry and philosophy persisted throughout all of what is a very complicated evolution of social knowledge. But, from a repository for almost all knowledge, philosophy has been left as a residual category which until today has continued to shrink in scope and, of necessity, to redefine its tasks periodically.

If this light survey of names associated with social knowledge at its various stages does nothing else, it alerts us to the fact that the emergence of a new name today is not unique. It occurs at a particular point in a history that has been under way for thousands of years and will undoubtedly continue. Each transition, from philosophy to natural and moral philosophy, to natural and moral sciences, then to the social sciences, and now to behavioral sciences, signals a stage in a truly linear movement in the nature and assumptions about our understanding of man in society. We may well suspect that some fundamental transformations have taken place today or are in mid-process.

The present

We are left with the problem, therefore, of seeking to understand why, at this particular moment in its history, a significant part of the social sciences has come to be called the behavioral sciences. In its origins it may well be that the concept can be considered an accident. During the Seventy-ninth Congress, when a Senate committee was exploring the need for a national science foundation to stimulate and provide funds for scholarly research, representatives of the social sciences worked hard for the inclusion of their disciplines within the scope of the proposed legislation. Whether through genuine error or design, there were some disapproving senators who, from the floor of the Senate, insisted upon talking of social science as socialist science. To abort the growth of further confusion, the phrase "behavioral sciences" is said to have been coined to refer to all living systems of behavior, biological as well as social. The underlying idea was that it would serve to identify those aspects of the social sciences that might come under the aegis of a foundation devoted to the support of hard science.[13] At about the same time the Ford Foundation was being organized, and, in seeking for an appropriate title for the section devoted to encouragement of the scientific development of social knowledge, the decision was made to call it the Behavioral Sciences Division. These two accidental forces converged to popularize the new name.

Whether or not the story about its origin is apocryphal, and however interesting speculation about the source of an idea may be, it is, of course, not decisive. Many ideas are born; only a few survive and spread. The task is to try to understand what there is in the nature of the present historical situation in research that has led social scientists to seize upon the new name in place of the much older and more familiar one.

In the adoption of this name by the various foundations, institutes,

---

[13] J. G. Miller, "Toward a General Theory for the Behavioral Sciences," in *The State of the Social Sciences*, L. D. White, ed. (Chicago: University of Chicago Press, 1956), pp. 29-65.

and departmental programs at universities,[14] the idea of behavioral science is applied to any social research concerned with a scientific understanding of man in society, regardless of the disciplinary umbrella under which it may find shelter. We hear talk about the study of religious behavior, economic behavior, political behavior, psychological behavior, and so forth. The concept applies well beyond the boundaries of the three so-called hard-core disciplines. But, as we have seen, at least from the point of view of helping to move these disciplines more quickly or surely in a scientific direction, the use of the concept would be superfluous. They were and are well known for their scientific commitments and have given little evidence of changing course. We might ask, therefore, whether in the broad sweep of the history of social knowledge the idea of the behavioral sciences does not foreshadow a new turning in the road, the beginning of a fundamentally new direction of development? The answer is clearly in the affirmative.

INTEGRATION OF THE SOCIAL SCIENCES

The new terminology reflects the fact that two new ingredients have been added to contemporary social research that will help to set it apart from all past eras. In the first place, never before has there been so great a demand for self-conscious attention to empirical theory at all levels of generality—middle range as well as general—that, in principle, can be reduced to testable propositions. In the second place, as part of this, the social sciences have been compelled to face up to the theoretical problem of locating stable units of analysis which might possibly play the role in social research that the particles of matter do in the physical sciences.[15]

In part, this turn toward empirical theory has been related to a hope that has never been completely lost from sight in the whole history of increasing specialization of knowledge and which appeared again in particularly strong form in the 1930's and 1940's. This was the idea that the understanding of man in society would be immeasurably enriched if some way could be found to draw the social sciences together into a basic unity. For a time integration of the social sciences became something of an academic will-o'-the-wisp, and, although it has lost its initial momentum, it has left a vital residue behind.

[14] The name appears in such titles as the Center for Advanced Study in the Behavioral Sciences at Stanford, California, the section of the Ford Foundation, now liquidated, that was known as the Behavioral Sciences Division, and the journals of *Behavioral Science* and the *American Behavioral Scientist*.

[15] For the analogy to physics, see "The Point of View of the Author" in *The Social Theories of Talcott Parsons, A Critical Examination*, M. Black, ed. (Englewood Cliffs, N. J.: Prentice-Hall, Inc., 1961), pp. 311-63.

Modes of integration

It turned out that scholars could conceive of integration of the disciplines as occurring at several different levels.[16] At the applied level one could bring the data of the social sciences together for the solution of whole social problems. Unification was to take place on the job, as it were. Housing, employment, peace, and the like were not to be seen as sociological, or economic, or political matters exclusively; adequate consideration of these would include the use of knowledge from a whole range of disciplines. Teams of specialists working together for practical purposes might thereby provide one kind of disciplinary integration.

A second kind might emerge through programs of research training. Students would be expected to address themselves not to a discipline but to social problems in the hope that they would learn to bring to bear on them the modes of analysis and data from any area of knowledge and research that seemed relevant and appropriate. The student was supposed to ignore the walls between the disciplines and to consider himself simply a social scientist. In such programs reference to the formal name of a discipline might be strictly taboo.

Related to but nonetheless different from this approach was a third kind in which it was felt that thorough training of a person in two or three disciplines might bring about a limited integration in the mind of a single individual. It would at least encourage such a fusion within the limits of the capacity of a single person to absorb and independently to synthesize a number of social fields. Here training was to be disciplinary in its orientation, but in the outcome two or more disciplines would be integrally joined.

Each of these three levels had something to commend it, each has left its mark on curricula for the training of social scientists, and each has helped to create a new self-image of the social sciences, at least with respect to their intrinsic interconnections. But none of these paths led toward any integral unification of the disciplines; at most, what was proposed was some kind of cross-fertilization or exchange of knowledge. They left the way open to search for a means of genuinely synthesizing the disciplines, and this has come to form a possible fourth level of integration.

The key idea behind this approach has been the conviction that there

[16] For some suggestions along these lines: L. Wirth, ed., *Eleven Twenty-Six, A Decade of Social Science Research* (Chicago: University of Chicago Press, 1940); C. Dollard, "A Middleman Looks at Social Science," *American Sociological Review,* 15 (1950), 16-20; B. F. Hoselitz, "The Social Sciences in the Last Two Hundred Years," *The Journal of General Education,* 4 (1950), 85-103; E. R. A. Seligman, "What Are the Social Sciences," *Encyclopaedia of the Social Sciences* (New York: The Macmillan Company, 1930), I, 3-8; W. Gee, ed., *Research in the Social Sciences* (New York: The Macmillan Company, 1929).

are certain fundamental units of analysis relating to human behavior out of which generalizations can be formed and that these generalizations may provide a common base on which the specialized sciences of man in society could be built. In place of some mechanical combination of the social sciences, this substituted an underlying basic science of behavior. Although, in reductionist vein, some have argued for psychology as the already existing basic science and others have put in a plea for sociology or anthropology or even political science, the main effort has gone toward the search for an entirely new foundation.

The expectation and hope that it will be possible to develop a common underlying social theory impels research in certain inescapable directions.[17] The most significant of these for our purposes is that it has led to the search for a common unit of analysis that could easily feed into the special subject matters of each of the disciplines. Ideally, the units would be repetitious, ubiquitous, and uniform, molecular rather than molar. In this way they would constitute the particles out of which all social behavior is formed and which manifest themselves through different institutions, structures, and processes.

Alternative units of analysis

We can concretize the meaning of this conviction if we glance at the way it has worked itself out to this point. As an example, in the case of Talcott Parsons, the Weberian derived notion of *action* seemed to provide the most fruitful unit out of which a common macrotheory might be constructed, one that would be serviceable to all of the social disciplines. Although the action frame of reference can thus be easily associated with the name of one scholar, there are other units of analysis that have been proposed but of which the paternity is multiple, diffuse, and converging. For some who have been strongly influenced by social psychology, the *decision,* or choice among alternatives has seemed to be the most promising unit. It even infected economics, which is the one social science that seemed invulnerable to change in this direction, so tightly knit and self-contained a theory did it already have. For others deriving from anthropology, *functions* of varying kinds supplied a rather broad and different kind of unit, somewhat slippery to handle, to be sure, but nevertheless a unit that could be utilized in many of the disciplines.[18]

Most recently, *systems* have made their appearance as a possible focus,

[17] Some of these directions are indicated in R. G. Grinker, ed., *Toward a Unified Theory of Human Behavior* (New York: Basic Books, 1956).

[18] R. K. Merton, *Social Theory and Social Structure* (New York: Free Press of Glencoe, Inc., 1949); M. J. Levy, Jr., *Structure of Society* (Princeton: Princeton University Press, 1952); K. Davis, "The Myth of Functional Analysis as a Special Method in Sociology and Anthropology," *American Sociological Review,* 24 (1959), 757-73.

beginning with the smallest cell in the human body as a system and working up through ever more inclusive systems such as the human being as an organism, the human personality, small groups, broader institutions, societies, and collections of societies, such as the international system. The assumption is that behavior in these systems may be governed by analogous if not homologous processes. General systems analysis is perhaps an even more ambitious effort than action theory to draw disciplines into a common framework, for it spreads its net over all of the sciences, physical and biological as well as social, and views them all as behaving systems.[19]

Let us disregard for the moment the particular answers designed to form the bridgework of a general theory. In its broadest sweep adoption of the label "behavioral sciences" symbolizes the hope that, ultimately, some common variables may be discovered, variables of a kind that will stand at the core of a theory useful for the better understanding of human behavior in all fields. In some vague way there has been added to this the feeling that psychology, sociology, and anthropology are the core sciences out of which such a theory may well arise.

This approach, it is clear, reaffirms a commitment to the assumptions and methods of empirical science, especially for those disciplines such as political science that have hitherto been reluctant to adopt them. But it goes further. It enriches this method by stressing the hitherto quite neglected theoretical component. Out of the whole scientific credo presented earlier, it is the theoretical tenet that is becoming magnified in our present historical period and that gives the scientific enterprise in the social disciplines the special character implied in the idea of behavioral sciences.

RELEVANCE TO POLITICAL SCIENCE

At this point, we may well ask: This is all very well for the current historical position of the social sciences as a whole, but what relevance for the meaning of the behavioral approach in political science can we attach to these trends? Bearing in mind the broader context in which our discussion has been taking place, we can now begin to draw together the threads so that we may more clearly see the basic theoretical implications of behavioralism in political science.

The point has already been made, that the literature on the subject in-

---

[19] A. R. Radcliffe-Brown, *A Natural Science of Society* (New York: Free Press of Glencoe, Inc., and Falcon's Wing Press, 1957); various articles in *General Systems,* Yearbook of the Society for General Systems Research, especially those by L. von Bertalanffy and K. Boulding in Vol. 1 (1956); Grinker, *Toward a Unified Theory.*

sists upon interpreting the behavioral approach in politics as the symbol of scientific method, the introduction of new kinds of data from the hard-core social sciences, and the like, each interpreter providing his own favorite emphasis. What all of these points of view fail to take into account in any serious way is the connection between the behavioral approach in political science and current trends toward theory in the general body of the social sciences, sparked, as this new theoretical tendency has been, by a strong interest in the integration of the disciplines. The behavioral aspect of the new movement in political research involves more than method; it reflects the inception of a theoretical search for stable units for understanding human behavior in its political aspects.

The dual revolution in political science

How does it come about that current interpretations of the behavioral movement in political science fail to appreciate this theoretical aspect? The neglect is understandable; it flows from the peculiar historical conditions under which political science finds itself today.

If we look again at the so-called hard-core sciences, especially psychology and sociology, we can see that, in them, the techniques of empirical research had been slowly maturing long before World War II. In fact, these disciplines had even had ample time to become overcommitted to the bare technical skills associated with a scientific approach. They had fallen into the bad habits of crude empiricism, the accumulation of data for the sake of the data themselves with relatively little consideration to matters of the relevance and broader significance of the findings. It was only late in the interval between the two world wars that they began to respond seriously to the idea that crude empiricism is not enough and to rediscover what some few had been long insisting upon, that relevance and understanding could be achieved only through the development of broad theory.

The reception of scientific method took place, however, long before the term behavioral science appeared on the horizon. Commitment to and engagement in scientific research, therefore, were antecedent to the relatively recent reawakening to the need for general theory relevant to human behavior. These disciplines had experienced a two-stage effect: first came scientific method and considerably later, as identified through behavioralism, theoretical concerns.

But in political science there has been no such orderly sequence of exposure to the different aspects of scientific method. From the point of view of the experiences of other social sciences, it has been undergoing two revolutions simultaneously. Political science has come to scientific method at about the same time as the social sciences as a whole have been shifting their emphasis from the methods of research alone to theory as well. In effect, a stage experienced by the core disciplines has been bypassed, or alternatively, two stages have been combined in one. Political science is in the process of absorbing the basic assumptions of scientific method at the same time as it proceeds to the equally trying task of giving meaning to the behavior studied by relating it to some empirical theoretical context.

What has been happening in political science is as follows. Political scientists have been adopting the assumptions and technical means associated with a science of society. At the same time they have been moving toward a behavioral approach. There is a danger in this formulation. It implies that behavioralism is different from scientific method, whereas it is only scientific method with a shift in emphasis to the substantive problems of concept formation and theory construction. But, because the behavioral emphasis has become so visible in other social sciences this label has been adopted to apply to both kinds of changes that are occurring simultaneously in political science. If we temporarily keep the technical imperatives of scientific method separate from the behavioral approach, we shall have a much better opportunity to understand the true character of the dual revolution currently under way in political science. By any logical criteria, of course, both these aspects, the technical and theoretical, are an integral part of scientific method.

The technical revolution

With regard to the reception of the technical aspect, surely little has to be said. Its origin lies in the early part of this century with the development by the 1920's of a series of conferences devoted to the new science of politics. But the full invasion did not occur until after World War II. The increasing prevalence in political research of the use of carefully devised interviews, survey research, technical methods for measurement, and the formalization of analysis in logical and mathematical symbols testify to the growing inroads that rigorous techniques are making. These have been fortified by the widespread introduction of instruction on the scope and method of political science and training in the use of mechanized procedures for recording and analyzing data. It is becoming increasingly difficult to keep up with political research unless one has at least a reading familiarity with the techniques being used. There can be little doubt about the nature and prevalence of this segment of the dual revolution.

The theoretical revolution

Although we may include this technical change as part of the behavioral movement, it seems sensible to do so only if at the same time we are equally conscious of the second revolution concurrently under way and which much more faithfully reflects pressures that have transformed other social sciences into behavioral disciplines. This revolution has involved the sharp consciousness that without far more concentrated effort on empirical theory our technical resources would be squandered.

In political science one may not always be conscious of the progress slowly being made with respect to the search for useful theoretical orientations under the very broad and poorly outlined behavioral umbrella. Perhaps this is because of the need to concentrate on the difficult and time-consuming task of refashioning the tools of research, learning new languages of analysis, and becoming familiar with the methods, data, and findings of related disciplines. But the long traditional preoccupation of political science with theory has left the political scientist peculiarly sensitive to the theoretical implications of the behavioral tendencies, and without being overly conscious about it he has been responding to these tendencies. In fact, when we pause to look at the inventory of empirically oriented theoretical ideas it is slight, as we might expect. But, given the very short time that the behavioral approach has been persuasive in political research, it may come as a pleasant surprise to discover that there are a respectable number of alternative conceptual approaches for the study of political life or some of its major segments. Not that these conceptual structures are fully developed or close to any ideal form. They do, however, constitute a beginning and a promise for the future.[20]

As in the case of the purely technical revolution, not all theoretical innovations have been confined to the postwar period. In a few instances during the interval between the wars empirical frameworks of analysis were proposed and elaborated. Catlin, for example, had turned to the "will" as his basic unit of analysis,[21] Merriam and others in the Chicago School had focused on power, and the group had been elevated to a central position. Since World War II many important additions have been offered, and these have helped to broaden the range of choice, to link political science to the main currents of research in other disciplines, and to enrich its theoretical insights. Undoubtedly, this search for adequate units of analysis—whatever the degree of awareness present—is preparing the ground out of which, in the none too distant future, may well emerge some minimal consensus.

We can obtain a better sense of the theoretical ferment that is accompanying the behavioral tendency and which forms a central part of it if we

---

[20] For an analysis of some of these, see the subtle and penetrating evaluations by Deutsch, *The Nerves of Government*.

[21] G. Catlin, *A Study of the Principles of Politics* (New York: The Macmillan Company, 1930).

examine more closely the kinds of units that have emerged. Until the 1940's Lasswell, virtually alone, had carried the burden of seeking to weave together theory and empirical research. At the end of World War II he was joined by Herbert Simon. Although little recognition has been given to the fact, in retrospect there can be little doubt that to Simon is due major credit for awakening postwar political scholarship to the role of empirical theory. The very title of his ground-breaking volume, *Administrative Behavior,*[22] showed how closely the new behavioral movement was linked with theory, in this case, in administration. At the same time it introduced the profession to the theoretical and empirical potency of his main unit of analysis, the decision.

The use of this variable as a central unit quickly spread to other areas of political science, aided as it was by its prevalence in other fields of social research as well. Decision-making has become the most generalized new concept in political research. It has been seriously and systematically adopted for research in community political structure and processes, in the empirical understanding of international relations,[23] and, at the formal level, in the logic of choice as expressed in game theories.[24] Simultaneously, research on voting, under the stimulus of social psychology, discovered a theoretical matrix for itself in the decisional concept.[25] The vote came to be interpreted not just as a rather unique kind of act in a democratic system but as one that brings to a head a special kind of decision that persons are expected to make in any number of contexts, such as committees and the economic market place as well as elections. The integrative quality of the decisional approach is most apparent at this level.

Furthermore, in a vague and general way, it has been adopted by large

[22] Herbert Simon, *Administrative Behavior* (New York: The Macmillan Company, 1957).

[23] Particularly in the works of Richard Snyder.

[24] See the writings of M. Kaplan, A. L. Burns, and R. E. Quandt and the symposium in *World Politics,* 14 (1961). For a particularly innovative and fruitful study dealing with the domestic life of political systems see W. H. Riker, *The Theory of Political Coalitions* (New Haven: Yale University Press, 1962). The following volumes of selected readings reveal the range and depth of theoretic and political gaming approaches: H. Guetzkow *et al.,* eds., *Simulation in International Relations* (Englewood Cliffs, New Jersey: Prentice-Hall, Inc., 1963); H. Guetzkow, ed., *Simulation in Social Science: Readings* (Englewood Cliffs, New Jersey: Prentice-Hall, Inc., 1962); M. Shubik, ed., *Game Theory and Related Approaches to Social Behavior* (New York: John Wiley & Sons, Inc., 1964).

[25] See the prevalence of this orientation in B. R. Berelson, P. F. Lazarsfeld, and W. N. McPhee, *Voting* (Chicago: University of Chicago Press, 1954); there is a brief comment on this in D. Easton and R. D. Hess, "Youth and the Political System" in *Culture and Social Character,* S. M. Lipset and L. Lowenthal, eds. (New York: Free Press of Glencoe, Inc., 1961), pp. 226-51, especially on p. 232.

numbers of political scientists in their research on general political processes; these tend to be described as the processes through which political decisions or public policies are made. As a result, it may be that the decisional orientation has begun to lose its original impetus, not because it has proved unequal to its tasks but rather because its points of major value have been largely absorbed into the mainstream of political research.

Units of analysis other than the decision have been proposed or elaborated for the study of political behavior. For example, although the concept of the group had been prominent in the interval between the wars, Truman elevated it to a new level of refinement and thereby made it eminently more usable for theoretical purposes.[26] Almond has sought to weave together the ideas of system, culture, function, structure, and action into a conceptual scheme designed particularly for comparative analysis and research.[27] Deutsch has organized a conceptual structure around the message and its networks as the major unit for a kind of analysis that leads toward a theory of political communications.[28] For many others associated with the behavioral movement the major unit has been at least some undefined but, nonetheless, real "behaving individual" in relationship with other behaving individuals, all of whom have determinable attitudes, motivations, knowledge, and values and who thereby constitute the universal "particles" of political life. In my own work, I have been exploring the utility of the system as the major unit, focusing on political life as a system of behavior operating within and responding to its social environment as it makes binding allocations of values.[29]

Although this list may not be exhaustive, it does illustrate the increasing attention being given to empirically or behaviorally oriented concepts in political research. Entirely aside from the merits of any one conceptual perspective, it is not easy to separate from a behavioral approach the fact that there is now available a considerable variety of alternative units from which to select and that there is a newly sharpened awareness of the need to articulate and to question critically the theoretical premises of empirical work.

Hence, too, we can better understand the efforts to redefine or describe

[26] D. B. Truman, *The Governmental Process* (New York: Alfred A. Knopf, Inc., 1951). In this respect the brief remarks by A. de Grazia should be examined in "Research on Voters and Elections," *Research Frontiers in Politics and Government,* pp. 104-34, especially p. 121.

[27] Almond, *The Politics of Developing Areas.* For a greater structural emphasis, see D. Apter, "A Comparative Method for the Study of Politics," *American Journal of Sociology,* 44 (1958), 221-37.

[28] K. W. Deutsch, *Nationalism and Social Communication* (New York: John Wiley & Sons, Inc., 1953).

[29] D. Easton, "An Approach to the Analysis of Political Systems," *World Politics,* 9 (1957), 383-400.

the limits of political science as a field of relatively self-contained phenomena. What some have felt to be fruitless and wasteful inquiries into the theoretical boundaries of our discipline have simply represented a groping toward at least the gross units in terms of which political life can be identified, observed, and analyzed; power, policy- or decision-making, groups, political communications, functions, systems are all such units. Slay the dragon of disciplinary redefinition as we may, it insists upon rearing its head in a new form each time and to higher levels of conceptual sophistication.

Behavioral research thus stands for a new departure in social research as a whole; it is the most recent development in a long line of changing approaches to the understanding of society. It means more than scientific techniques, more than rigor. This alone would indeed mean *rigor mortis* as its critics from the traditional points of view, both classical and institutional, have been so quick and correct to indicate. The behavioral approach testifies to the coming of age of theory in the social sciences as a whole, wedded, however, to a commitment to the assumptions and methods of empirical science. Unlike the great traditional theories of past political thought, new theory tends to be analytic, not substantive, explanatory rather than ethical, more general and less particular. That portion of political research which shares these commitments to both the new theory and the technical means of analysis and verification thereby links political science to broader behavioral tendencies in the social sciences; hence, its description as political behavior. This is the full meaning and significance of the behavioral approach in political science.

TWO

*Political Life as a System
of Behavior*

No one way of conceptualizing any major area of human behavior will do full justice to all its variety and complexity. Each type of theoretical orientation brings to the surface a different set of problems, provides unique insights and emphases, and thereby makes it possible for alternative and even competing theories to be equally and simultaneously useful, although often for quite different purposes. The conceptual orientation that I am proposing—systems analysis—is one that stems from the fundamental decision to view political life as a system of behavior. Its major and gross unit of analysis will be the political system.

Systems Analysis: An Overview

What kinds of commitments might be inadvertently undertaken if political life is characterized as a system of behavior and the implications of this description are pursued diligently? The answer to this question will be the subject of our discussion in this section.

Much research has assumed the existence of a system of political activities; it might indeed be argued that it is impossible to conduct coherent research without making such an assumption. This in itself may be enough to justify characterizing such approaches as forms of systems analysis. Hence, at times, the label "systems analysis" has been applied to numerous modes of analysis such as game theory, functional research, or equilibrium theory.[1] The idea "system" itself has become so popular in the last decade that the most unlikely approaches have sought authentication under its wing. It is one of the thunderous concepts of the century, starting in the natural sciences and quickly reverberating not only through the social sciences but on into such apparently remote fields as education, art, and aesthetics.[2] However, the fact that the term has become so popular (if not the victim of a scholarly fad) has contributed more to the obscurity of its meaning than to the clarity of its use. I propose, therefore, to give this theoretical orientation a much more specific and restrictive meaning. This will make it possible to distinguish the commitments of the approach I shall be elaborating in this volume from many other kinds of research in which the idea of system may loom large or appear frequently.[3]

Systems analysis as conceived here will be built upon the following general premises. Only the first two of these need it share with other modes of analysis that revolve around the concept "system" as a primary axis.

1. *System.* It is useful to view political life as a system of behavior.
2. *Environment.* A system is distinguishable from the environment in which it exists and open to influences from it.

[1] "In the last two decades we have witnessed the emergence of the 'system' as a key concept in scientific research. Systems, of course, have been studied for centuries, but something new has been added. . . . The tendency to study systems as an entity rather than as a conglomeration of parts is consistent with the tendency in contemporary science no longer to isolate phenomena in narrowly confined contexts, but rather to open interactions for examination and to examine larger and larger slices of nature.

Under the banner of *systems research* (and its many synonyms) we have also witnessed a convergence of many more specialized contemporary scientific developments. Where those interested in systems research gather we are likely to find representatives of every scientific discipline who have become expert in such diverse fields as communication theory, cybernetics, computers, decision theory, value theory, the theory of games, operational gaming, and organizational theory. These research pursuits and many others are being interwoven into a cooperative research effort involving an ever-widening spectrum of scientific and engineering disciplines. We are participating in what is probably the most comprehensive effort to attain a synthesis of scientific knowledge yet made." R. L. Ackoff, "Games, Decisions and Organizations," *General Systems,* 4 (1959), 145-50, on p. 145. See also A. Kuhn, *The Study of Society: A Unified Approach* (Homewood, Ill.: Richard D. Irwin, Inc. and The Dorsey Press, Inc., 1963).

[2] For example, see L. Meyer, *Emotion and Meaning in Music* (Chicago: University of Chicago Press, 1956).

[3] To appreciate how broad and varied a field might be included under the category of systems analysis see articles in the Yearbook of the Society for General Systems Research, *General Systems.*

3. *Response*. Variations in the structures and processes within a system may usefully be interpreted as constructive or positive alternative efforts by members of a system to regulate or cope with stress flowing from environmental as well as internal sources.
4. *Feedback*. The capacity of a system to persist in the face of stress is a function of the presence and nature of the information and other influences that return to its actors and decision-makers.

It is the third and fourth premises that fundamentally distinguish this kind of systems analysis from other approaches to the study of political life that at least implicitly interpret it as a system of behavior. In general, systems analysis, as I shall conceive it, takes its departure from the notion of political life as a boundary-maintaining set of interactions imbedded in and surrounded by other social systems to the influence of which it is constantly exposed. As such, it is helpful to interpret political phenomena as constituting an open system, one that must cope with the problems generated by its exposure to influences from these environmental systems. If a system of this kind is to persist through time, it must obtain adequate feedback about its past performances, and it must be able to take measures that regulate its future behavior. Regulation may call for simple adaptation to a changing setting in the light of fixed goals. But it may also include efforts to modify old goals or transform them entirely. Simple adaptation may not be enough. To persist it may be necessary for a system to have the capacity to transform its own internal structure and processes.

From this perspective, systems analysis of political life responds most sensitively and rewardingly when questions are posed that seek to unravel the processes through which a political system is able to cope with the various stresses imposed upon it. In its ultimate returns this mode of analysis will enable the investigator to understand more fully the way in which some kind of political system in a society manages to persist in the face of stresses that might well have been expected to lead to its destruction.

The bare minima by way of major concepts that need to be understood for the analysis of political life in the systems framework are system, environment, feedback, and response. From this elementary initial structure of concepts, I shall argue that is is possible to evolve a relatively more complex and, hopefully, logically coherent framework for an analysis of political life that will raise a new order of problems for consideration.

THE ISOLATION OF A SYSTEM

What is meant by the idea of a system of behavior? Does political life constitute such a system? Since in recent years it has become quite commonplace to refer to politics as a political system, it might appear trivial, if not superfluous, to ask at this late date whether it is helpful or appropriate to apply the term to political life. But the fact is that, however frequent the usage, only in the exceptional case is the concept employed in a strictly theoretical sense implying specific theoretical commitments. In most cases it is just a handy notion, popular and apparently simple, to refer to the range of phenomena that in earlier days might have roused a different terminology, such as politics, government, or the state. Yet, the concept contains within it major theoretical implications. By exploring them I shall be able to prepare the grounds on which it will later seem reasonable if not compelling to interpret political life as an adaptive, self-regulating, and self-transforming system of behavior. The concept "system" when rigorously employed already implies a systems analysis.

Empirical and symbolic systems

System as a concept may be used in two different but related senses. First, it may refer to the empirical behavior which we observe and characterize as political life. These are the objects of observation, the things that, as students of politics, we wish to understand and explain. We can speak of this phenomenal reality as the empirical or behaving system with respect to which we hope to develop some explanatory theory.

Second, the concept may refer not to the world of behavior but to the set of symbols through which we hope to identify, describe, delimit, and explain the behavior of the empirical system. System here applies to a set of ideas or theory; hence we may call it a symbolic or theoretical system. In empirical science, as compared to such deductive sciences as mathematics, the value of every symbolic system lies in the adequacy with which it corresponds to the behaving system which it is designed to explain. In this sense a causal political theory would constitute a symbolic system which has as its point of reference the behaving system we call politics.

It is of the utmost importance to keep these two kinds of systems distinct. In this work I shall be speaking of the empirical or behaving political system with respect to which I shall be in the process of seeking to develop a theoretical system. My problem will be the following: If we are to understand the way in which the behaving political system functions, what is the nature of the commitments we must make at the conceptual level, once we attribute systemic qualities to the actions that we shall subsequently identify as constituting political life?

Simultaneously, therefore, I shall be called upon to use as my objects of reference both the behaving and the symbolic systems. At times, I shall wish to talk about the implications at the theoretical level of the assumptions that I shall make; this is fundamentally a logical task, tempered as it may be by our knowledge of how people do interact politically. At other times, I shall find it necessary to speak about the extent to which the concepts and the generalizations employing them correspond to the empirical world, that is, to the empirical system. It is my hope that it will be clear from the context whether my object of reference is the empirical or the theoretical system. The concept "political system" will identify the behaving system and the concepts "structure of analysis," "conceptual framework," or "theory" will be used to refer to the symbolic system.

Natural and constructive empirical systems

Although I have been speaking as though political life does form a system of behavior about which we can develop a system of theory, what evidence have we that this is indeed the case? Is it a supposition that common sense compels us to accept without further inquiry? Is it not possible that political interaction may lack the properties that we may intuitively associate with anything that we could reasonably call a system? These are not rhetorical questions. They raise the problem of when we may conceive any set of interactions to form a system.

Fundamentally there are two ways in which these questions could be answered. We might hold that whether or not a set of interactions constitutes a system will depend upon the extent to which they naturally cohere. From this point of view, systems are given in nature; as natural phenomena, it is the task of the social scientist to discover the ones that do exist if he wishes to observe systems in operation.

But it is possible to adopt a different position and to argue that all systems are constructs of the mind. We might maintain that it is pointless to try to distinguish so-called natural from nonnatural or nonexistent systems. In this interpretation any aggregate of interactions that we choose to identify may be said to form a system. It is solely a matter of conceptual or theoretical convenience. This hardly seems like a defensible position. Yet, as it turns out, this is the only position that will enable us to avoid more problems than the concept would otherwise create.

The problem

The first position, that systems lie in nature waiting for the observer to discover and explore them, is the more usual assumption and seems to accord with ordinary common sense. There would seem to be little reason for identifying some aspect of life as a system of behavior unless we believed that it "really" was a system. On this premise, nature provides us with sets of interdependent actions such that a change in one part will be likely to affect what happens in another part. Included within a system will be only those actions that display a coherence and unity or constitute a whole. Modification in any part of these must have determinate repercussions on other parts. If not for this connectedness of the parts, there would be little point in identifying the behavior as a system. As one strong advocate of this view phrases it, "a natural system, then, is a conceptually isolated portion of phenomenal reality (the system separated from the rest of the universe which is then the total environment of the system), consisting of a set of entities in such relation to one another as to make a naturally cohering unity."[4] It is the fact that the interactions under scrutiny seem to share a common fate, that the elements move together, that permits and even compels us to acknowledge that they form a system.[5]

From this point of departure it would be quite erroneous to posit that systems may be any set of elements brought together for one or another research purpose. Specifically, to argue that there are no natural systems but that any set of social interactions makes up a system would in effect leave it possible to hold that political strife among the Bantu in Africa, for example, and party politics in the United States form a single political system.

Stated in this way, this position sounds either very naive or even nonsensical. However free we are in principle to attribute any meaning we choose to a term, it would seem that we would be better advised to look for those political relationships that cohere or are interconnected in some material way before we call them part of the same system. We would then quickly see that the Bantu form political systems quite separate and different from that of the United States and that aside from international contacts they would be best studied as units at the same level and not as part of the same unit.

It seems so straightforward and unquestionable an interpretation to insist upon reserving the concept "system" for a unit that incorporates patterns of behavior that are interrelated in nature, that one may well wonder why it is even worth mentioning, especially at such length. There is, however, good reason for thus seeming to belabor the obvious. What appears to be simple and intuitively given turns out to be considerably more complicated theoretically. If we insist upon assuming that systems are natural in the sense in which they have been discussed and that sets of political interactions must have the properties of natural coherence before we can call them systems, in the end we shall expose ourselves constantly to the challenge of whether the patterns of behavior to be identified later as a political

---

[4] Radcliffe-Brown, *A Natural Science of Society*, p. 20.

[5] D. T. Campbell, "Common Fate, Similarity and Other Indices of the Status of Aggregates of Persons as Social Entities," *Behavioral Science*, 3 (1959), 14-25.

system constitute a "genuine" system. We cannot push ahead theoretically until we have removed every reasonable doubt about the status of system as a concept of analysis.

LIMITATIONS OF THE CONCEPT "NATURAL SYSTEMS"

The idea of natural systems can in reality serve little theoretically useful purpose. Three arguments stand in the forefront to support this conclusion.

In the first place, if we assert that our major and gross units of analysis are natural systems, this would in no way help us to locate such systems. We would still have the task of taking any set of political relationships and exploring their connectedness. If we find that they are mutually determined, we can conclude that we have fortunately made the correct selection of variables at the beginning. If, on the other hand, upon investigation we find that the relationships we had expected do not appear and the elements selected are independent of each other, we reject the set as being randomly related. We conclude that they must have formed a nonsystem all the while.

Our decision to designate the system as natural or not does not aid us in the least in establishing the determinacy of the relationships. Whether the struggle for power among the Bantu in Africa covaries relevantly with partisan politics in the United States can be ascertained only by investigation. To say, therefore, that in adopting systems as our gross unit of political analysis, we are compelled to be careful to select only natural political systems has little operational significance in helping us to find and isolate such a system or to test its coherence. We must still go through the motions of discovering whether or not the elements of our system have sufficient interrelationships to form a presumed "natural" system.

In the second place, the search for natural systems would also create a virtually insurmountable difficulty. Where the components of any set of behaviors are tightly—as well as significantly—connected, there is no problem. If a change in one of the variables immediately leads to some change in another, or where a small change in one introduces large modifications in another, the systemic ties are transparent. Thus we have no difficulty in linking expressions of voter preference and the power of the Democratic or Republican parties in the United States as part of a single system. But where the components of a presumed system are loosely associated, where a considerable change in one has negligible or no discernible effects on the other, the answer does not come so readily. As the ties between variables become increasingly attentuated, at what point does the nature of the set as a system disappear and emerge simply as a random collection? The line would have to be drawn somewhere, and it is difficult to know where it would be theoretically, much less empirically. It opens the door to interminable dispute as to whether or not a set of activities "really" forms a system, and we shall find this dispute to be a totally unnecessary, spurious, and distracting issue.

In the third place, not all covariance would intuitively meet the criteria of a system. It is possible to discover many kinds of relationships in political actions for which no meaningful explanation can yet be offered. It leaves open the question as to whether the existence of what is only an apparent interdependence would thereby transform the elements into a system of some kind. Depending upon the subjective judgment of two different observers, the same variables would constitute a member of the two mutually exclusive sets, systems and nonsystems, at least until evidence was adduced to demonstrate the genuineness of the interdependence.

Alternatively, would it be necessary in order to have a natural system to demonstrate that these relationships among variables that do exist are relevant for an understanding of the operations of the system? The search for so-called natural systems seems to solve little in this respect as well. It would still leave us saddled with the crucial problem of establishing the interconnectedness of a set of variables and demonstrating their theoretical relevance or meaningfulness.

DIVIDENDS OF THE CONCEPT "CONSTRUCTIVE SYSTEMS"

Interesting versus trivial systems

From a methodological point of view, it would appear to be possible, profitable, and, therefore, sensible to abandon the notion that political systems are given in nature. We can simplify problems of analysis enormously, without violating the empirical data in any way, by postulating that any set of variables selected for description and explanation may be considered a system of behavior. At the outset, whether it is a system given in nature or simply an arbitrary construct of the human mind, is *operationally* a pointless and needless dichotomy. What commands our attention is the need to decide whether the set of activities is an interesting one, in the sense that it is relevant and helps us to understand some theoretical problems, or whether it is worthless or trivial from this point of view.

Where the selected parts of political life are relevant, show some degree of interdependence, and seem to have a common fate, we can say that we have an interesting and useful system from the point of view of understanding the way in which political systems are likely to operate. Where the selected aspects of political life seem to have little to do with each other and knowledge of one does not help in understanding the other, we may still say that they constitute a system of political behavior; however, the only thing that can be said about its component elements is that they are independent of each other—what happens to one does not affect the other. From the point of view of seeking generalizations about political life, they form a relatively trivial and uninteresting system. It is not a matter, therefore, of having found a political system in the one case and in not having done so in the other. Rather, we can consider that we have systems in both instances, an interesting one and a trivial one.

This is not an evasive manner of defining the concept; nor is it just a minor objection. On the contrary, this way of classifying systems does have two distinctive advantages for our approach to political analysis. It avoids and eliminates all possible dispute about whether or not the object of our analysis is or is "really" not a system. Any set of political elements we wish to consider a system automatically becomes one. The significance of this remark may not be clear at the moment but it will be strikingly obvious once we begin to identify the elements of the empirical political system.

In addition, this position permits us to change our minds about the importance of systems. It enables us to say that one that was totally uninteresting because we could see very little interrelationship among its parts has suddenly become significant, new data having suggested possible connections. We can do this without having to go through a superfluous process of arguing that a nonsystem has suddenly been transformed into a system.

*Criteria for the selection
of constructive systems*

In criticism of this position, it may be asked: What is there to prevent us from stating that everything in the world is related to everything else, thereby combining all social life into one grand system? If we did this, it would at least spare us the difficult task of having to decide about which elements to include in an apparently arbitrary system. There is, of course, nothing to prevent us from doing this. We could say that all kinds of political behavior in the world, wherever they are found, are to be aggregated into a universal, omnibus system.

Although there is no logical reason why this could not be done, it is more significant to point out that there is no positive reason for doing so. There does not seem to be any theoretical or substantive ground for assuming that such a procedure would be an aid in understanding the way in which people behave politically. We delimit the system under observation, or select a particular set of political elements from among all possible combinations that might easily form a system, because on various theoretical grounds (to be discussed in subsequent chapters) some variables seem to have greater significance in helping us understand the political areas of human behavior. Our task will be to establish criteria of selection, as indicated by research interests, so that we may carve out a limited range of activities from the total phenomenal reality of politics. These we shall designate as a political system, and they will compose our gross empirical unit to be analyzed.

For other purposes or from some other kind of theoretical posture than the one to be adopted here, it is not only conceivable, but likely that some other overlapping set of variables would probably be selected to constitute the system at the focus of attention. There is no reason why there should be any foreordained, unalterable set of variables, the examination of which will answer all significant political questions. It is also completely beyond our present comprehension to expect that we shall ever achieve the millennial condition of isolating and describing fully and definitively the major elements of political life that contribute to its variations in time and place. No other science, however rigorous its methods or ambitious its goals, has ever come close to this state; there is no reason to think that political science will be a lone exception.

The apparent permissiveness, if not overindulgence, with regard to each scholar's whim, suggested by this position, is quite deceptive. Even though we may arbitrarily decide to consider a duckbilled platypus and the ace of spades as our political system—and logically there is nothing in the way of doing so—conceptually it would be pointless. We are confronted with the task not of making a capricious choice of variables, but of selecting that combination which on the basis of experience, insight, and past research seems likely to give us the most economical and most valuable understanding of why people behave in politics in the way that they do. Unfortunately, it is impossible to specify in advance those criteria of choice that would assure the best possible selection. But this kind of "payoff," in the form of increased understanding, acts as a constraint upon choices and militates against the indiscriminate selection of activities out of which we would build the systems of behavior to be analyzed.

That there are such constraints is demonstrated by the whole history of physics, for example, which can be shown to be one of successive redefinitions of the system that constitutes the major unit of analysis. By alternatively adding, rejecting, and revising its constituent elements, the system called the atom has been expanded and reconceptualized until today it is practically unrecognizable when compared with earlier versions.

Similarly, even without the further modifications that will be suggested in later chapters, the political system has already been expanded and modified in American political research over the last half century or more. From a view of it as being composed of formal or legal structures with attendant and incidental activities, it was expanded to include informal activities within the formal structure, interest groups, and motivational or personality dimensions.

In recent years many new ways of viewing old forms of political activities and many additional kinds of behaviors have been added to those already included within what most students of political life would accept as part of a political system.

Logically, therefore, we are free to include within a political system any range of actions at all; substantively, in the light of the objectives of research with regard to political life, we are limited by our conceptions of what is significant and relevant for an understanding of why people act in the way that they do in political situations. Because of this obvious constraint on the selections of things for inclusion or exclusion, in practice it is not an arbitrary matter, nor is it ever a matter of whim, as to how a political system is to be defined.

Perhaps in this context alone it might be meaningful to speak of political life as a natural system. In this event all that could be meant is the following: Through experience, insight, and wisdom it has become apparent that, given the kind of questions to which answers are being sought, the observer will probably not be able to resolve them without considering a specified set of variables. It is likely that these will fall somewhere within a range of phenomena with respect to the relevance of which most students of political life would agree. These comprise a natural system in the sense that they appear to cohere significantly. Without them it does not appear likely, on *a priori* grounds, that an adequate explanation of the major aspects of political phenomena could be obtained. The interconnectedness of the variables seems clear and obvious, at least until dispelled by subsequent inquiry; in this way alone may they be considered "given" in or by nature. But this is just another way of saying that they form what I have been calling an interesting, as against a trivial, system.

The universality of system as a concept

In further criticism of this broad interpretation of the meaning of the concept "system" itself, it might be argued that since everything and anything, in isolation or combination, may be considered a system, by definition there can be no set of variables that does not form such a system. Since all things fall into the class of systems, there can be no class of nonsystem. If nothing is omitted, the concept "system" can itself have little meaning.

It is not a matter as to whether it is valid to utilize the concept in this way. *Concepts are neither true nor false; they are only more or less useful.* The appropriate question relates, therefore, to the utility of so liberal a concept that it includes all or any part of the whole social universe as possible systems.

It has been pointed out with respect to this very concern that the social sciences would not be the first to find so universal a category to be of central utility in its analyses. The concept "system" corresponds in some ways to the idea of mass in physics. For the physicist, all physical things have mass; there is no place in their conceptualization for physical things that do not have mass. In thus attributing mass to all physical things, there is no intention to treat this statement as an hypothesis or a description subject to factual validation. Rather, it simply reports the intention on the part of physicists to treat their subject matter in a unified way.[6]

The same interpretation applies with regard to the function of system as a concept in social research. It is a way of orienting ourselves to our data at the very least; and as I have intimated and as I shall expand very fully, it also provides crucial leads into the analysis of our subject. However, as a way of looking at social life, if it should prove to hamper rather than facilitate efforts to understand and explain political interaction, at that point it can be discarded for more fruitful ways.

We know from the variety of contexts in which we find the idea "system" used today that it certainly does not narrowly dictate any single mode of analysis, even as a significant orienting concept. Its adoption though will impose some broad constraints on the kinds of analyses that are logically and consistently possible. Furthermore, if it does not impose strict limits, it does make possible and suggest a range of theorizing that would otherwise be quite impossible. This is its major and easily neglected value; the concept opens up more interesting doors than it closes, no mean achievement in science. There would be little point in adopting such a concept unless we were able to do something with it substantially different from what could be done without it.

As we shall quickly see, by conceptualizing political life as a system and by delineating it distinctly from its environment, we shall be able to introduce a range of matters for analysis that are otherwise very difficult to grapple with. Yet they represent an order of problems that will prove to be exceedingly illuminating, if not inescapable, in seeking to understand the way in which political life functions. At the very least, this mode of conceptualization will enable us to interpret political life as an open system and thereby to pose questions with regard to the kinds of exchanges that such a system has with its environment, to the way in which the members of the system respond to these exchanges, and to the determinants of these dynamic processes.

[6] I have borrowed this illustration from R. C. Buck, "On the Logic of General Behavior Systems Theory" in *Minnesota Studies in Philosophy of Science,* H. Feigel and M. Scriven, eds. (Minneapolis: University of Minnesota Press, 1956), I, 223-38 on p. 227. The author, however, uses the same illustration for opposite purposes!

THREE

The Theoretical Status of Systems

Regardless of whether social systems are artificial constructs of the mind or symbolic reproductions of naturally cohering phenomena, we cannot take it for granted that the typical elements that all systems share are intuitively or readily known. This is not a question of the substantive characteristics that distinguish one type of system from another, such as a political system from an economic one. We shall examine this subject in due course, but we have a prior matter to consider. Is it even possible to conceptualize any social system in such a way that it can be readily distinguished from other systems? What are the basic elements of which political systems, like other social systems, are composed?

THE UNITS OF A SYSTEM

Initially we might be prone to answer this question by pointing out that the basic element common to all social systems is the individual person. Intuitively this seems the most reasonable response. If we could indeed stop here and imagine social systems as being made up of entities such as the whole biological person and all his behavior, we would rouse few conceptual complications. A system composed of interacting human beings, palpable, visible and whole, certainly does not stretch the imagination. Yet, strangely enough, in this common-sense interpretation lurk unusual ambiguities that are easily ignored or glossed over.

We begin to encounter conceptual difficulties if we are asked to entertain the notion that it may be impossible to adopt the human being as the major unit for analyzing social systems. To insist on this would seem to do serious violence to the phenomenal reality. Nevertheless, I shall be arguing that all social systems are composed of the interactions among persons and that such interactions form the basic units of these systems. A political system is not a constellation of human beings that is selected out for investigation. It is a set of interactions isolated from other kinds of interactions in which the human being is engaged. Clearly, such an interpretation and its implications are not immediately obvious to common sense nor can we expect them to be readily acceptable.

What was said in the last chapter quickly and easily removes at least one stumbling block. Since we have already discovered that any set of things may be termed a system, we are relieved of the need to consider whether such a set of interactions forms a so-called genuine system. All systems are of equal validity in our terminology, as systems, although all may not have equal utility for purposes of understanding political life.

Even though doubts about the empirical status of a system need not hold us up, a further complication does occur. Frequently the actions of one system, such as a political system, are not found in relative isolation. They are imbedded in or enmeshed with other interactions and scarcely distinguishable from them empirically, at least by ordinary observation. This certainly creates even greater difficulties in seeking to abstract them out in order to analyze them as a separate although interrelated system.

What these comments do is to raise for discussion a major question with regard to the theoretical status of any social system, particularly as it bears upon the political system. Is it useful or empirically correct to conceive of a political system as being composed of biological persons interacting with each other? Ought we rather view a political system as a set of interactions, entered into by human beings, but nevertheless temporarily abstracted from the other nonpolitical kinds of behavior in which they are engaged? Are there perhaps two different kinds of systems? The one, membership systems, would encompass the whole concrete person as the basic entity; the other, analytic systems, would refer only to the abstracted interactions in which persons engage, interactions that have been factored out of the total web of behavior of which they are part.

I shall propose that the value of and necessity for intellectually separating out such a set of interactions is that we shall be able to use this as a tool to simplify reality. As students of man in society, it is obvious that we are not able to deal with all of a person's behavior in an undifferentiated and total way. We need to develop concepts that enable us to view the special interactions in which we are interested, such as the political, as though they occurred separately for the moment. Empirically, the interactions will certainly occur as an inextricable part of other interactions and will probably be conditioned by them. But to analyze any one set of interactions, it will be mandatory to abstract them from the whole matrix of behavior within which they occur. This is what will be meant when I shall refer to a political system as analytic. All social systems must be interpreted as being analytic in character. It will be crucial, therefore, to explore the grounds for believing in the necessity of this interpretation. This is an unavoidable preliminary step on the road toward the construction of a conceptual apparatus for the understanding of political life.

THE ANALYTIC CHARACTER OF ALL SOCIAL SYSTEMS

The plausibility of membership systems

What justification is there for asserting that social systems must be analytic in character? To appreciate the kind of intellectual commitments that this view requires, let us explore what is involved in the alternative position that might hold that at least some social systems, or subsystems, are concrete membership systems rather than analytic ones.

Common sense would seem to verify that we have membership systems and that these are fundamentally different at least from those systems that might be composed of interactions diffused throughout society and abstracted from the individuals who are engaged in them. As a membership system, a religious system might include all the persons, as such, who are members of religious organizations. As an analytic system, presumably it would include all those interactions in which any individuals in a society engage and that could be designated as religious regardless of whether they occurred in an organized context or in a strictly religious setting. Conceivably the analytic system could be much broader than the membership system since many persons could engage in religious behavior without belonging to religious units.

Even posing the problem in this way lends considerable credibility to this distinction between systems: that memberships systems are not analytic because they deal with the whole persons as the entities of the system. But this is apparent only. Before we can accept what seems transparent to common sense, we need to determine explicitly whether each type of system has equally clear referents in the phenomenal world. If we are driven to conclude that one or the other does not have and, in principle, could not have such referents, it would undoubtedly have considerably less usefulness in the development of an empirical science.

Society as an all-embracing suprasystem

We can best approach an understanding of the theoretical status of a political system if we begin with the most inclusive social unit we know, a society. Regardless of how we might define the term for substantive purposes, it at least incorporates all other social systems and therefore refers to the overarching, inclusive, suprasystem in which a group of biological persons participates. In this sense, society constitutes a unique kind of social system. We would find it impossible to specify the whole range and variety of interaction in which the component persons engage. In referring to society, we are conceiving of all behavior undifferentiated as to type, what we might call the apperceptive mass of observations present to our senses. As a concept, society calls attention to the gross mass of conceptually unorganized social interactions that we might perceive if we were able to take in the whole of a society, literally, in one glance.

However, once we undertook to digest our mass of crude sensations, we would begin to impose some order on them, differentiate those we are interested in, and give them labels. If we did this for purposes of understanding the way in which society functions, we would, in effect, be isolating different systems of behavior. To put this in a formal and more general sense, in the way I am using the term here society encompasses the social behavior of a group of biological persons, conceived in their totality. A social system identifies some narrower aspect or part of the social interactions in which these biological persons engage. These represent the various roles in which persons engage so that the same biological persons may turn out to play different social roles.

For scientific purposes, over the course of time it has appeared useful to identify different kinds of interactions, each of which has appeared to be significant in explaining the functioning of societies. These are so well known that they scarcely need justification. We have sorted our religious, economic, fraternal, educational, political, cultural, and similar kinds of behavior. Where the purposes seemed to indicate it, each of these kinds of interactions has been viewed separately as systems. Since such systems do not represent the totality of the interactions involved in a society, but only parts of them that have been abstracted out of the apperceptive mass of behavior, I am suggesting that these systems are analytic in character. Political interactions constitute one kind of such systems.

The empirical image of an analytic system

To this point, aside from the terminology, there might seem to be little with which to cavil. But a major hurdle blocks the easy acceptance of this perspective on the theoretical position of system as a concept. It is one thing to verbalize that political interactions constitute an analytic system. It is another to attempt to visualize what this means or to conjure up an empirical image of such a system. Is it possible to transform this image into a phenomenal model? If not, how are we to grasp the meaning underlying the notion of analytic system?

If we had begun with the idea that a political system is a system of biological persons, there would be little difficulty. It is relatively easy to imagine a small group of administrators in an agency, many of whom are located in a contiguous area called an office, as a system of persons. In principle, even in the case of a larger agency with spatially dispersed offices, given the will and equipment, we could readily imagine collecting the whole group as a unit, putting it into a conveyance and transporting it as a unit to a new location. There is a clear physical aspect to the group that makes it easy to visualize as a system much along the lines of the physical systems with which we are familiar in the natural sciences. There is an apparent intrinsic unity and cohesion to the group determined by the physical presence of persons, their proximity, common structure, and shared purpose.

This view is reinforced by the fact that, when we speak of the administrators in the agency, we seem to have in mind more than just the actions in which the members of the agency engage. It is the biological persons themselves that we seem to be considering. In principle, we visualize each individual as he interacts with others and all of them interacting together and persisting through time to form a simple and very satisfying image of a physical system.

Even if we turn from the organized group to modern differentiated societies, although it is not so simple a conceptual task as with regard to the kind of organizations we have been referring to, nevertheless, it does seem to make good sense initially to think of biological persons acting in relationship to each other in a cohering system of behavior. In differentiated societies specialized roles appear in the political system that seem to occupy, if not the whole of the interactions of the biological person, at least a sufficiently large share of them so that a person is identified by the name of the role itself. Thus we have politicians, representatives, administrators, judges, political leaders, and the like. We do not have to stretch the imagination very far to consider them all, collectively, as being more or less related to each other in an interacting system. Because of the degree of role specialization, it even seems transparent that such a system would consist of the whole person and might well be interpreted as a membership system of behavior. It would be the biological person who is the member of a political system composed of these and other roles.

Ambiguities with respect to fused social structures

The imagery of a system begins to break down when we turn away from specialized roles or organized groups to the vast complex of political activities that are diffused throughout each society, however differentiated its political structure. For example, even in modern highly structured societies many members may engage in political activities outside of any formal role that is designated as political or as part of their behavior in roles that are distinctly nonpolitical. Arguing about political policies, making demands, agreeing to support a candidate, criticizing public officials, all are forms of political participation that need not and frequently do not occur within the context of a political organization or in any formal political setting. It is also customary for individuals to pass political opinions or even solicit political support for a point of view while they are engaged in the actions associated with some clearly nonpolitical role. Businessmen may talk politics over the dinner table or during negotiations of a business character; educators may exchange political opinions in process of resolving purely educational matters.

Here the imagery of a system may appear more difficult to grasp. If we conceive of a system as a physical model in which we have a group of biological persons in persisting interaction through membership in an entity (such as a formal organization, large or small) or through communication at a distance, a political system would not always meet the test. It is impossible to collect all the political actors together and transport them to a new location, as apparently seems to be so for an organized group, without simultaneously shifting the locus of the whole network of social systems called a society. When moving the political actors, we would at the same time have to move the same biological persons who are engaged in economic, religious, educational, and other kinds of behavior that constitute a society. We would be transporting not only a political system, but all other systems as well. We cannot empirically or physically always separate out those interactions that we might agree to call political and view the political actors as a group completely or largely independent of the economic and other types of actors. The result is that if we designate all of these formal and informal political activities, that is, all political interactions, as the components of a political system, such a system seems to become less real or less tangible than a system apparently composed of a specifiable number of biological persons, as in the case of an organization or other formal group.

When we turn to nonliterate and many traditional systems, where the areas of activities do not command the degree of differentiation and specificity of modern societies, the problem of empirically identifying a political system, or even other kinds of social systems, becomes infinitely more complex. The chief in a tribe may be the head economic decision maker as in cases where on his authority decisions are taken about when and where the group is to move in its search for food. He may also be the ritual leader, the main arbiter of disputes, and the focus of festive occasions. All kinds of activities may center in the one individual. For that matter, all individuals in the society may perform most tasks; the members of the society need not identify the separation of tasks through role specialization. At most, empirically, all activities are inextricably interlocked in a few limited roles such as kinsman, follower of a chief, or paramount chief.

There are many intervening degrees of differentiation or fusion in roles other than the two extreme cases already illustrated—namely, modern structurally differentiated societies and small traditional tribal systems. But they do demonstrate that political life need not be sharply demarcated from other kinds of behavior in all societies. Even in modern societies not all political activities are as easily isolated as in the case of the well-defined and named political roles. A citizen who purchases a loaf of bread and at the same time exchanges opinions with the clerk about a local candidate for political office is contributing some activity to two kinds of systems, the economic and the political. Underlying the highly differentiated levels of political activity in modern society, there still remains a deep substratum of behavior that occurs as part of the general, undifferentiated activities of any member of a society. One may talk politics to an acquaintance at church on Sunday morning; important political attitudes may be transmitted unobtrusively at the family dinner table. Yet we are not prone to include the church or family, except under special circumstances, as directly political organizations and, therefore, as structural components of a political system.

The whole fabric of a society, as in the case of the highly politicized Western societies and in the very many nonliterate tribal groups, may be permeated with political interactions of this sort. They occur in settings that are otherwise not differentiated politically and therefore could not be included as a whole within the constituent elements of a political system. Yet, these actions have potentially significant consequences for the political life of the society and certainly could not be omitted from consideration as part of a political system, at least without violating every canon of good sense. If, in order to make the idea of a system palatable, we had to insist upon having as its members a group of biological persons who interact exclusively or largely in a political framework, it is clear that we would not be able to include such interactions as part of a political system.

The analytic character of all systems

One way of handling this difficulty conceptually would be to say that what we have are two different subtypes of systems: a membership or entity as against an analytic system. The membership system would consist of biological persons in physically separate organizations; the analytic system, of sets of interactions spatially dispersed, diffuse, or imbedded in other kinds of behaviors. The value of such a twofold classification is that it would signalize the obvious importance of organized actions in political life.

However, if in setting up this classification, we thought that we had distinguished two systems dissimilar in their theoretical status, we would be committing a gross conceptual error. Membership and analytic systems are in fact both analytic systems of significantly different subtypes, to be sure, but, nonetheless, of the same theoretical status. They differ with respect to the concentration or emphasis of a political orientation; membership groups will usually have a higher degree of differentiation and specialization, both in space and time, of their political interactions.

To see the elements they have in common as systems, let us look again, and more closely, at these well-defined clusters of political roles that we call organizations. In modern societies, because of the division and specialization of labor in politics as in other social areas, we have numerous organizations and institutions in which the quantity and saliency of political activities are so great that these structures are recognized as primarily political in nature. The fact that they are given political names identifies them as structures heavily freighted with political consequences for the society. Political parties, legislatures, various kinds of interest groups, or courts are unmistakably part of political life.

But because of the very lack of ambiguity about this relationship to politics, what is often lost from sight is that the members of these structures are not identical with the whole biological person. The very concept "member" reflects the fact that we are drawing attention to only certain aspects of the biological person's behavior and including it as part of the organizational system. Other aspects of his behavior we may choose to ignore entirely or treat only as relevant external conditions. The roles of members in a political system frequently contain behavior that has consequences for other areas of society. Political parties raise and spend money and to that extent contribute to the production of goods and services in the economy. They also provide contexts for the pursuit of friendship and thereby add to the structural integration of the society.

What is true for the political party is equally true for other differentiated political roles and structures. Every political institution has multiple consequences for varied aspects of society. An institution such as campaigns has effects, if only very marginal, on the economy. The money a person gives to his favorite candidate or party cannot be spent on other goods and services. The reason we apply the term political to certain organizations, institutions, or roles is simply that the major *consequences* of the behavior of these units are directed toward the political rather than the economic, religious, or other areas of life. But even where we find such a strong emphasis in the direction of the political significance of the behavior, we cannot conclude automatically that all the activities have only political consequences or that they are all political in nature. Some are nonpolitical, even if negligibly so.

Practically, it may not be of great significance to point out the obvious economic relevance of the behavior of political parties, as indicated. The diversion of funds for political campaigns is undoubtedly of little significance for the state of the economy. Conceptually it has far greater importance. It indicates that, in effect, when we look at highly specific and differentiated types of behavior, as in a political organization, we factor out of the total apperceptive mass of actions only those that are political. That we identify some set of behavior in this way must not deceive us into overlooking the fact that we have abstracted a part from the whole and labeled the whole in terms of this basic part. In other words, even organizations that are beyond doubt dominantly political in nature, such as a political party, are abstractions from the whole of behavior in which a person engages and, therefore, are analytic subsystems. So-called membership systems are really not systems of biological persons, but of specialized roles. In this sense they too are analytic systems. In referring to such systems for purposes of research, we are abstracting out of the total pattern of behavior in which the biological person is engaged that part that relates to his actions in his organizational roles.

This is also precisely what we do when we look at nonorganizational forms of political behavior or when we seek out the political aspects of interactions taken in organizational or institutional settings that are not primarily political in character. We abstract out of the total interactions in which a person engages those that are oriented to politics, regardless of whether he is acting in the role of a member of a lineage group, the director of a corporation, or a distinguished member of the artistic world. For the moment we may disregard any question about the criteria in terms of which a selection of what is or is not political is to be made. We shall turn to this shortly. We can assume, for present purposes, that we are able to establish some agreeable criteria. In that event we must recognize that all those interactions that meet the test are and can only be analytically derived, regardless of whether they occur in a specifically political role or as an inadvertent and concealed aspect of some role apparently alien to political life. Theoretically, their status is that of abstractions from the total situation. In no case does the study of social behavior deal with the total undifferentiated mass of actions in which a biological person engages. All action, as perceived by the observing social scientist, by definition must be analytic in nature.

THE EMPIRICAL REALITY OF ANALYTIC UNITS

Does this mean that because a political system cannot avoid being analytic, it must in some sense be less concrete or less observable than the apperceptive mass of behavior of the biological person? Just because a political system is an abstraction of one defined kind of behavior among many other kinds does not leave it any the less empirically observable than the crude undifferentiated mass of behavior of which it is part.

The analytic characteristic of the political system does not affect its empirical status. It refers only to the fact that for purposes of theoretical treatment political activities will be differentiated and temporarily abstracted from all other kinds of activities. But we are still dealing with observable behavior.

This approach will not lead us to ignore the other kinds of behavior out of which the abstraction is made; they will have important consequences for the political aspects of the total behavior. Indeed, we shall see that they make up the social environment of a political system. We will need to take into account the interaction among the different analytic systems by which political behavior may be shaped. We can devise specific analytic tools to make this systematically possible and the effort to do so will engage a good part of subsequent chapters. Here I wish to stress the point that in examining that analytic part of social interaction that we shall call political, we shall be looking at concrete, observable interactions.

In conclusion, then, we may say that if by membership system we mean systems of biological persons useful for research purposes, there are no such systems in social science. All systems of behavior are analytic. Some are more differentiated, specific, and integrated for limited purposes; these we may call organizations, systems of roles or membership systems in this restricted sense of the term. Others are diffuse and undifferentiated, enmeshed in other analytical kinds of interactions. But regardless of the structural expression of behavior, all systems must be interpreted as abstractions from reality, empirically relevant but isolating only a part of the phenomenal world.

The theoretical status of a political system is that, like all other social systems, it is analytic but nonetheless empirical in character. If we now recall our discussion of what we mean by a system, we are relieved of any need to dispute whether political interactions, as an analytic set, really do or do not constitute a system of behavior. Such a discussion would be superfluous. Since by definition any set of interactions may be labeled a system, the appropriate question to pose is whether a particular kind of abstracted behavior, to be identified shortly as political, constitutes a scientifically interesting one. Will it compose a sufficiently adequate and comprehensive body of referents to enable us to answer some of the major problems that have been raised historically with regard to political research or that appear currently relevant for an understanding of political life? If these abstracted interactions do not, this will certainly not "prove" that they do not constitute a system. It can only suggest one of a number of alternative plausible explanations: that we have lacked sufficient insight to isolate the critical political variables for inclusion within our system and, therefore, within our range of interest; or that the conceptualization of political life as a system is not particularly helpful in leading to an understanding of the phenomena in which we are interested.

FOUR

The Identification of the Political System

The premises adopted to this point with regard to the characteristics of social systems are twofold. Any set of variables may be selected to represent the system at the focus of attention. Society, as the most inclusive social system, is the only one that encompasses all the social interactions of the biological persons involved. Every other social system, including the political system, isolates only some aspects of the total behavior and must, therefore, be analytic in nature.

In terms of the mode of analysis under discussion in this volume, political life will be interpreted as a system conceptually distinct from other systems in a society. Those interactions that fall outside of a system may be designated as the environment in which a political system exists. In introducing the analysis in these terms, I shall be implying that there is some kind of boundary between a political system and its environment.

As we shall see, this is a central idea. Once it has been established, it will permit us to speak of the exchanges or transactions that take place between a system and its environment. A major task in constructing a detailed theory would consist of efforts to identify these exchanges and account for the way in which a political system manages to cope with the problems that they create for the persistence of a system. To put the matter in a slightly different but theoretically more general way, it would be pointless, if not impossible, to push ahead in our analysis and to conceptualize political life as an open and self-regulating system, as I shall, unless it were feasible both analytically and empirically to distinguish a political system from its total environment.

Several questions will have to be answered if we are to demarcate a political system from other kinds of systems. First, what is included within a political system, and how are we to identify it? Second, what can we possibly mean by speaking about a boundary between analytic systems? Third, what is excluded from a system, to be interpreted as part of its environment? These questions will command our attention in this and the succeeding chapter.

CRITERIA FOR IDENTIFYING A POLITICAL SYSTEM

How shall we distinguish those interactions in society that we shall characterize as the components of a political system? This is one of the critical steps in examining the dynamics of political life. In describing the general property of interactions to be considered part of political systems, we automatically establish the kinds of behavior that will be omitted. It is essential that our criteria of inclusion omit no vital elements. If we cannot adequately account for the way political systems function, the major incentive for isolating a political system will have been defeated. Yet for purposes of research, political science cannot study all phenomena; the real world must be reduced and simplified in some way. Inevitably this opens up the danger that some elements of major importance may inadvertently be excluded.

This possibility is ever present since, as we have seen, there is no ultimate test in the form of its "naturalness" of what elements are to be included as constituting a political system, aside from their anticipated explanatory power. But this gives us very little apparent advance guidance; explanatory utility is always an *ex post facto* kind of test. In the initial selection of the properties of those elements to be identified as characteristic of political life, we must be guided by what we have come to know about political life through the study of history (or past experience) and through the observation of ongoing systems (or present experience). Any potential caprice inherent in insight and subjective judgment is ultimately curbed by the fact that persons starting from different premises will normally be led to construct different theoretical models. In the criticism and discussion of these alternatives, selective and corrective processes occur, one hopes, that will lead to the improvement of our theoretical formulations and, thereby, of our understanding of how political systems function.

Interactions as the units of a system

In the traditional study of political life behavior that roughly corresponds to what I shall be calling a political system has been characterized in many ways, combining or oscillating between the needs of the time and the predilections of the investigator. Political life has been described in such terms as the study of order, power, the state, public policy, decision-making, or the monopolization of the use of legitimate force. In *The Political System* and elsewhere[1] I have discussed a number of these points of view at length and have considered reasons for rejecting them, not as wrong of course, but as less useful at our present level of knowledge than the following alternative.

In its broadest context the study of political life, as contrasted with economic, religious, or other aspects of life, can be described as a set of social interactions on the part of individuals and groups. Interactions are the basic unit of analysis.

Simple as this formulation is, it militates against a tendency still strong in political research to move directly to the particular structures, whether formal or informal, through which political interactions manifest themselves. The study of legislatures, executives, parties, administrative organizations, courts, and interest groups, to select a few, still dominates the initial approach that political scientists typically take toward their data. With the broadening of the focus enforced upon political science by the discovery of the developing nations and their vastly different political structures, political scientists have looked with diminishing favor upon this emphasis on formal and informal structures. But in spite of this, we have continued to force the study of these newly discovered political systems into the Procrustean bed of traditional assumptions.

From the point of view of the analysis being developed, structure is definitely secondary, so much so that only incidentally and for illustrative purposes need discussion of structures be introduced. Certainly no attempt will be made to consider political structures in any systematic way. The assumption will be that there are certain basic political activities and processes characteristic of all political systems even though the structural forms through which they manifest themselves may and do vary considerably in each place and each age. Logically and temporally prior to

[1] D. Easton, "Political Anthropology" in *Biennial Review of Anthropology*, B. J. Siegel, ed. (Stanford, Calif.: Stanford University Press, 1959), pp. 210-62.

the examination of such structures, it is vital to explore the processual nature of these political interactions. This stress on the processes of political interactions lends a dynamic character to political analysis, as we shall see, that must be absent from any premature and undue emphasis on the forms or patterning of political behavior.

The test of political interactions

Furthermore, what distinguishes political interactions from all other kinds of social interactions is that they are predominantly oriented toward the authoritative allocation of values for a society. Political research would thus seek to understand that system of interactions in any society through which such binding or authoritative allocations are made and implemented.

Briefly, authoritative allocations distribute valued things among persons or groups in one or more of three possible ways.[2] An allocation may deprive a person of a valued thing already possessed; it may obstruct the attainment of values which would otherwise have been obtained; or it may give some persons access to values and deny them to others.

An allocation is authoritative when the persons oriented to it consider that they are bound by it. There are many reasons why members of a system may consider themselves bound. Knowledge of these would help us to understand variations in the processes of different systems. Important distinctions can be attributed to the acceptance of allocations as binding on the grounds of fear of the use of force or of some severe psychological sanction, such as imprecations in primitive systems or social opprobrium in more complex ones. Self-interest, tradition, loyalty, a sense of legality, or sentiments of legitimacy are additional significant variables in accounting for a feeling of obligation to accept decisions as authoritative. But regardless of the particular grounds, it is the fact of considering the allocations as binding that distinguishes political from other types of allocations in the light of the conceptualization that I shall be using.

PARAPOLITICAL SYSTEMS

The political systems of groups

If political research confined itself to the investigation of the way in which binding allocations were made, regardless of the context, it would result in casting its net so broadly that it would include vast ranges of behavior normally not viewed as strictly political. Authoritative kinds of allo-

[2] I have examined this interpretation of political science in detail in *The Political System.*

cations are made in all types of groups, ranging from the family and lineages through fraternal clubs to religious, educational, and economic organizations. We might well ask whether, in my conceptualization, these too must represent political systems or whether, at the very least, they incorporate political systems as an aspect of their total behavior.

There is no absolute prohibition against adopting so catholic an interpretation of politics that it would permit us to discover political systems in all other social groups in addition to society itself. It is true that in doing so we might be violating the normal use of the term. Political research is not usually or especially concerned with the processes within groups for their own sake. Only insofar as they can be related to the larger political processes in society have the internal workings of organized groups—"private government"—attracted the attention of students of politics in the past. That this is not customary in the traditions of political research need not in itself deter us.

Indeed, we might be able to make a sound case for including aspects of the internal social interactions of all subgroups in society as examples of political systems in their own right. As Charles Merriam put it, "obviously there is governance everywhere—government in heaven; government in hell; government and law among outlaws; government in prison."[3]

Like the more inclusive society of which they are part, groups do make allocations that are accepted by their members as binding. In such subgroups as families, churches, or fraternal organizations we find constitutions, competition for control among dominant and aspiring elites, and pressure groups or factions. These subgroups have available, as well, potent sanctions to enforce compliance with their allocations, such as coercion through excommunication, ostracism, blackballing, or violence, as in the case of criminal organizations. Under the prevailing norms the bulk of the membership may consider the invocation of such sanctions to be legitimate. Clearly, there are parallel structures and processes present in the broader political system in or adjacent to which the subgroups find themselves.

Although, as I have suggested, for some purposes it may be useful to broaden the concept "political system" to include these aspects of groups and organizations, for our purposes they need be considered only analogous to rather than isomorphic with the political system of a society. For this reason, examination of the structures and processes related to the authoritative allocation of values in organizations and other groups can be quite helpful in shedding new light on the structures and processes of the more inclusive societal political system. To hold otherwise would run counter to an increasing body of evidence pointing up important similarities. The study

[3] C. Merriam, *Public and Private Government* (New Haven: Yale University Press, 1944).

of organizations and small groups in terms of their power relationships,[4] decision processes, and communication flows has provided insights and concepts for the analysis of the broader political system.

But similarities are not identities. There are theoretically and empirically significant differences. In order to keep the societal political system unambiguously differentiated from less inclusive systems, I shall refer to the internal political systems of groups and organizations as *parapolitical systems* and retain the concept "political system" for political life in the most inclusive unit being analyzed, namely, in a society.

Differences between political and parapolitical systems

However similar the processes and structures of parapolitical systems may be to the societal political system, they differ substantively in at least two important respects. To begin with, parapolitical systems are, at most, aspects only of subsystems in a society. They are subsystems of subsystems. The members of no parapolitical system either accept or are expected to accept the responsibilities for dealing with the major problems generated by the fact that an aggregate of persons live together as a society, share some aspects of life and are compelled, thereby, to try to resolve their differences together. These responsibilities transcend the scope of any single organized group. Parapolitical systems are concerned only with problems of authoritative allocations within the group.

To be sure, differentiation of function may take place so that some groups acquire greater roles in the resolution of differences. A royal lineage may pre-empt all claim to political office in a tribal political system or a political party may dominate in the political processes of a modern society. In these cases the nature of the intragroup or parapolitical system will help to determine the way in which the group behaves externally in the societal political system. However, the internal political systems through which values are allocated within the groups themselves—the clan or party, to continue the illustration—deal with a range of problems narrower than those arising in the political system of the society in which these groups may participate so potently. The very existence of an organized group testifies to some limit on its concerns and responsibilities as compared to the more inclusive society of which the group is part.

It is not just that society includes more people. It is rather that as parts of a societal political system these groups participate in the processes through which all and not just a segment of the problems of living together

---

[4] D. Cartwright and A. Zander, eds., *Group Dynamics, Research and Theory* (New York: Harper & Row, Publishers, 1953); S. M. Lipset, M. A. Trow, J. S. Coleman, *Union Democracy* (New York: Free Press of Glencoe, Inc., 1956).

as a society fall within their purview. The societal political system, therefore, possesses a range of responsibilities that are far broader in scope than those of the parapolitical systems within the subgroups of a society.

This does not mean that the societal political system undertakes authoritative allocations with respect to all aspects of living together or all the differences that arise. The fundamental fact confronting all societies is that scarcity of some valued things prevails. It leads inevitably to disputes over their allocation. Varying with each society and with each age within any one society, many of the conflicting demands over scarce values will be settled as the result of the autonomous interaction among individuals and groups themselves.[5] With respect to such matters, society in fact may not and may not be expected to intervene in any formal or special way. Aside from providing at least a minimal skeleton of order in most cases (in some primitive systems, however, there is no equivalent to the king's peace or chief's order), no society attempts to impose its settlement on all differences among its constituent individuals or groups.

But where differences are not resolved independently and where they are also perceived to be excessively disruptive of the prevailing ideas of order and justice, every society provides for processes through which special structures either aid in achieving some regulation of the differences or impose a settlement. These differentiated roles we identify through such concepts as rulers, government, authorities, chiefs, and clan elders.

This is not to say that society as a whole need benefit from these settlements according to a given set of criteria of what is just or good. The order or regulation may, and typically does, favor one component group more than another. Nor need the settlements empirically contribute to order. They may well result in aggravating the situation, inducing violence and chaos, perhaps ultimately assuring the destruction not the integrity of the society. The nature of the consequences for society is always an empirical matter that cannot be prejudged, although given sufficient information it may be predictable. Regardless of the consequences of a settlement, however, the major difference between a political system and a parapolitical system lies in the range of matters with which the former deals as compared with the latter. In fact, this is one of the meanings implicit in the statement that societal political systems are more inclusive than any or all parapolitical systems taken singly or in the aggregate.

A further major distinction between these two kinds of political systems is that the powers available to the societal political system for attempting to

---

[5] D. Easton, *A Theoretical Approach to Authority* (Stanford, Calif.: Department of Economics, Stanford University, 1955). Report No. 17 for the Office of Naval Research.

regulate differences are usually broader, corresponding thereby to its greater range of responsibilities. In both parapolitical and political systems there may be differentiated roles through which the major responsibilities for managing the political affairs of the groups are exercised. In both cases we may call the occupants of these roles, the authorities, although in modern societies we are more apt to call the roles for the parapolitical systems by different names such as an executive committee, a governing council, or a board of directors. But unlike their counterparts in parapolitical systems the authorities in political systems are differentiated by the special capabilities that they possess to mobilize the resources and energies of the members of the system and bring them to bear upon broad or specified objectives. These they are able to do in the name of the society and with the authority obtained through the acceptance of their position in the society. The governing body of no parapolitical system has such a capacity to speak in the name of society, the most inclusive social system, unless it happens to coincide with the authorities of the societal political system.

Because of their responsibilities, oriented as they are to society as a whole, the authorities typically have special instruments at their disposal to reinforce their capacities and to support the expectations that they will help to bring about settlements of differences. Thus, except in periods of rapid change or crisis, their settlements will come to be viewed as binding by most members of the society, even by those who may oppose the settlements or who may not otherwise be affected by them. Special norms of legitimacy, tradition, or custom have universally evolved as informal sanctions at the disposal of those burdened with such responsibilities. In many cases these are supplemented by formal sanctions in the shape of instruments for the imposition of force and violence to ensure conformity with allocations that are made. Perhaps the most comprehensive and powerful instruments with these consequences have been devised in association with the growth of the form of the societal political system that we have come to call the state. In these the legitimate use of force and violence is lodged exclusively in the hands of those who act in the name of the whole society.[6]

It is true that groups such as the family or formal organizations may expect compliance from their members and may be able to impose severe sanctions for disobedience. But the legitimacy of the kind of settlements they impose is recognized and accepted only by their own members, and not usually or necessarily by most members of the society itself. If the scope of the claims to obedience by such groups or organizations extends beyond

---

[6] For evidence that political systems may endure even if there is no legitimate monopoly of physical enforcement, see I. Schapera, *Government and Politics in Tribal Societies* (London: C. A. Watts & Co., Ltd., 1956), p. 217. He indicates that among Bushman and Bergdama tribes the chief is devoid of such powers; self-help is the sole means for enforcing the rules.

their own membership to the whole of a society with respect to the major problems of a shared existence, either they will come into conflict with the existing governing structure or they must become identical with that structure.

It would be perfectly feasible to undertake a comparative analysis of political and parapolitical systems or to consider them both as the primary referents of a conceptual analysis. We might then classify each as a different species of the same genus. In this way there is little doubt that much could be learned about the structures and processes through which binding allocations are made and implemented for groups of persons. Such a procedure, however, could easily lead us to gloss over the very two differences among these types of systems on which I have just commented.

As we shall see even more clearly in a later chapter, the primary goal of political analysis is to understand how political systems manage to persist through time. If we wished, we could build upon the experience of parapolitical as well as political systems, but the differences between the two types of systems as already indicated, together with the different kinds of environments in which they exist, militate against the fusion of the two types.

Instead, I shall exclude the internal political systems of groups and organizations from my frame of reference, and I shall choose not to consider them co-ordinate with the more inclusive political system of a society. Rather, I shall include within the conceptual structure to be developed only societal political systems. They, at least, have in common the same scope of responsibilities as defined and similar specialized capacities to mobilize and commit the members of a society. This does not mean that the analysis will be without significance for parapolitical systems. Indeed, there is considerable evidence in the literature on organizations and in some developing political research that a similar mode of analysis, appropriately modified, helps to illuminate some of the internal problems and boundary exchanges of subsystems in a political system.[7]

The decision to confine the analysis to political systems has the added virtue that, without sacrificing theoretical criteria of selection, it conforms to a long tradition of political research. This has dictated that the subject matter of political research, at its most general level and broadest context, should embrace the most inclusive political system of a society.

Although accord with tradition is no virtue in itself, the tradition has not arisen by chance. It reflects the continuous recognition that no society could survive without providing for some processes through which authoritative allocations could be made, if and when differences arise with regard to valued things. Contrary to inferences that might be made from anthro-

[7] J. C. Wahlke et al., The Legislative System (New York: John Wiley & Sons, Inc., 1962), especially Chap. I.

pological discussions of so-called stateless or acephalous societies, there is good evidence to illustrate that even in the case of the smallest bands of Bushmen, consisting of no more than a small extended kinship group of some fifty persons, some things that can be called "government" exist.[8] At least a headman may have a special role. In such societies the absence of differentiated structures for the performance of the tasks involved in making and implementing binding allocations is no indication of the absence of political systems.

From the perspective that I am adopting, therefore, political allocations are made in all kinds of empirical social systems short of society itself: families, extended kinship groups, business firms, trade unions, political parties, or churches. Each of these social subsystems contains sets of activities that we can designate as its political system. The conceptual structure to be developed here certainly has relevance for an understanding of the operations of these parapolitical systems. Much could be learned by indiscriminately assimilating parapolitical and political systems, in my terminology, into one class of objects. But for the reasons outlined the concept "political system" will be reserved for those roles and interactions relevant to the authoritative allocations for a society as a whole.

THE BASIC STRUCTURAL UNIT OF ANALYSIS
IN THE POLITICAL SYSTEM

The political system is the most inclusive system of behavior in a society for the authoritative allocation of values. As we know, this behavior refers only to an aspect of the total interactions in which the biological persons in a society engage. How then are we to refer to these persons as they engage in political interactions of one sort or another? It would be helpful to be able to reserve the concept "person" to refer to the whole apperceptive mass of interactions in which the biological unit engages. What we need is an analytic device that will enable us to select out that aspect of the person as he engages in politics.

Let us restate this in the formal terminology of contemporary social research. We are seeking a generic term that will be useful in referring to the political role as distinguished from the economic, religious, or other general roles of a person. We have numerous concepts to refer to specific political roles but none to identify the political role as such. With regard to some political systems, we are able to speak of the subjects or citizens and thereby include within our discussion all persons as they act in their political

---

[8] See the references in Easton, "Political Anthropology," and Schapera, *Government and Politics in Tribal Societies*, p. 217 and elsewhere.

roles. For tribal systems we may speak of the kin or the man of a particular chief. In these terms we do have some concepts of very general scope, but each of these concepts—citizen, subject, kin, man in terms of follower—is specific to the diffuse role as played by persons in societies with typically different kinds of political systems. Subjects usually refer to the person in an authoritarian kind of system, citizen to those in the modern territorially oriented kind of state, kin to tribal societies and the like.

In searching for a generic concept to identify the role of a person who is part of a political system in any kind of society and any kind of system, I have found it useful to adopt the simple term "member." I shall refer to the members of various political systems. By this I shall mean the most general role of a person in a given society with respect to political life. It indicates only that we shall be looking at a person from the point of view of his participation in political life in some shape or form, if only as the passive recipient of the results of the active behavior of others to which he orients himself. The value of the term is that it leaves entirely open the specific nature of the role. The member of a political system may be a citizen or subject, kin or alien, ruler or ruled. He may act individually, as part of an aggregate such as a political elite or public, or as a member of a group such as an association, legislature, or party.

What must be constantly borne in mind with respect to "member of a political system" as a concept is that this does not refer to the whole biological person or all his interactions. It is definitely an analytic category. It selects out or abstracts only those aspects of his behavior that are more or less directly related to the authoritative allocations of values for the society. The concept "membership" of a political system will correspondingly identify collectively the persons in a society as they pursue their political roles. It will be a quick way to avoid the circumlocution of speaking of all biological persons with respect to the political aspects of their social interactions.

A political system, therefore, will be identified as a set of interactions, abstracted from the totality of social behavior, through which values are authoritatively allocated for a society. Persons who are in the process of engaging in such interactions, that is, who are acting in political roles, will be referred to generically as the members of the system. If the conceptualization of political life as a system impels us to identify the major and general elements of the system, it commits us equally to the need to describe what it is that lies outside of a system. In fact, as the next chapter will reveal, it raises the question of whether and how it even makes sense to talk about things external to an analytic system.

FIVE

The Environment of a Political System

If a political system is to be identified in the way we have done it in the previous chapter, the other side of the coin could be expected to reveal those things that are not included within the system. But if we are to entertain the notion that there are things outside of a system, latent in our minds must be the complementary idea that there are boundaries of some kind that demarcate a political system from whatever is not included within it. If that is so, in one way or another we must be able to indicate the nature of the boundary that tells us when something is happening in the environment or nonpolitical sphere. At the very least, such a boundary should not be conceptually ambiguous. It should have sufficient empirical referents so that positive clues are available to tell us when a person is acting as a member of a political system and when his interactions occur outside this area.

Furthermore, once the idea of a boundary between systems is introduced, it should make sense to say that if something happens in the nonpolitical arena, it may influence the political system. An exchange will have taken place across the boundaries of the two systems. Except for this possibility, there would be little point in seeking conceptual clarity with respect to the environment of a political system.

AMBIGUITIES IN THE CONCEPT
"SYSTEM BOUNDARIES"

It seems reasonable to impose conceptual requirements such as these in connection with systems terminology. Yet when we look at the phenomenal systems, we encounter certain apparent difficulties and ambiguities. To consider a relatively simple obstacle, by way of illustration, are families, as structural units, to be excluded from political systems? If we were considering solely primitive, nonliterate societies, we might not be predisposed to do so too hastily. There, interactions within and between both nuclear families and extended kinship groups are highly charged with political content; this was equally true in earlier days among the aristocratic classes of many European societies. In at least two ways most families in modern societies continue to play a part in politics: through the contribution they make to the socialization of their own maturing members with respect to political attitudes, knowledge, and values; and in a diffuse way through the continued molding of the political attitudes and opinions of adult members. But the bulk of a family's activities relates to matters that cannot be labeled political. Yet because of its transparent participation in the vital area of political socialization and attitude formation, does this suggest that the family as a structure should normally be placed within the boundaries of the political system? To do so would be counter to common sense.

In a like vein, we might point to the investment policies and other activities of powerful financial houses in an industrialized society. These have at times been critical for the political destinies of a political party and government, as in the case of the influence presumably exercised by the Bank of England during the financial crisis of the Ramsay MacDonald Government in the thirties.[1] For that time are we to consider that the Bank of England and its specific actions lay inside the boundaries of the English political system? We would probably decide against inclusion of this structure on the grounds that the Bank was primarily an economic institution and therefore fundamentally part of the economy, especially since at the time it was privately dominated. Does this signify that if we are to be consistent, we must view a structure like this as part of two systems or that we at least ought to see it as oscillating between the political and economic systems?

At worst, this imagery seems to invite excessive reification or unpalatable analogizing; at best it confronts us with the real difficulty of decid-

[1] R. Basset, *Nineteen Thirty-One: Political Crisis* (London: Macmillan & Co., Ltd., 1958), Chap. 4, especially p. 62.

ing how we are to describe the boundaries of a political system so that we know what we can usefully include and exclude. For that matter, it raises the even more serious question as to whether we can intelligibly continue to speak of the boundaries of a system of interactions and of movement or exchanges across such boundaries.

The Significance of System Boundaries

If the questions as to whether boundaries were real or mythical, simplifying or complicating, had little consequence or relevance for our subsequent analysis, there would be little point in pursuing the discussion any further. We shall find, however, that the idea of exchanges between a political system and its environment plays a critical role in the theoretical approach being developed. The concept "boundaries" will represent an essential analytic tool, and this for two reasons.

Closed and open systems

In the first place, an explicit conception of boundaries will aid us immeasurably in simplifying, interpreting, and understanding the way in which changes in the environment are communicated to a political system and the way in which a system seeks to cope with these influences. It is obvious that many changes in a political system may be owing to factors internal to it. Its own form of organization may be the source of major difficulties, such as those attributed to the separation of powers in the American political system.

Other significant kinds of stress may derive from the fact that a system is open to influences from its environment. Although this is an inescapable observation, an empirical truism need not always provide the groundwork for a theoretical analysis. For some purposes it is often necessary and useful to violate what is known, temporarily at least, in order to build a simplified model even if it bears only a remote resemblance to reality. It is entirely possible to conceive of a mode of analysis that would follow some models of physical systems and interpret political life as a closed system, one that conceived it to be isolated from the influences of its environment. Such an interpretation would require us to account for what happens in a political system solely in terms of its internal activities.

This is not quite so farfetched as it may seem. In the past considerable research with respect to political life did leave the impression that insufficient account was being taken of the parameters of political behavior. Personality, culture, and social structure, three of the major parametric systems, have only episodically been used as central explanatory variables until recent years. But no political scientist could neglect the obvious effects of at least some of the nonpolitical aspects of social life.

Nevertheless, if for initial analytic purposes we were to adopt the assumption that a political system is entirely closed, we would be forced to conclude that the system would have to move toward what could be called maximal social entropy. We would be rather hard put, however, to describe just what is implied in the notion of a political system "running down" in any sense comparable to its use in the physical sciences from which the ideas of closed system and entropy are borrowed.

As meaningless as the term might be for a political system, it does serve the vital purpose of forcing us to conceptualize the nature of the relationship between a system and its environment. That is, it raises what has been a latent assumption to a conscious level so that we recognize that we have indeed been conceiving of political life as an open system. Because this notion has been latent, its implications have not been fully understood nor has its theoretical significance been clear or fully exploited.

Once we raise the notion of an open system to the level of theoretical consciousness, it impels us to clarify the meaning conveyed by the idea of a system as distinct from its environment. To say that a system is open to outside influences makes sense only if we can distinguish inside from outside. But we cannot do this satisfactorily except by examining the properties of a presumed boundary that separates the two. At a later point the logic behind the idea of an open system will also make it necessary to seek to develop concepts that will enable us to handle an analysis of the exchanges between a system and its environment. At that time we shall find the ideas of inputs and outputs invaluable for this purpose. Here again the idea of exchanges or flows of effects would make little sense unless we were able to think of boundaries across which such transactions took place.

Identification of dependent variables

In the second place, the adoption of boundaries as a concept will also represent a strategic step toward the simplification of reality, an essential condition for any scientific research. It will provide us with a criterion for determining which politically important elements need to be explored in depth as our major dependent variables and which may be accepted as given in the form of external variables. Each of these types of elements, the internal and the external, will be crucial for an understanding of our problems concerning political systems, but each will have a different theoretical status in the conceptual model that we are in the process of constructing.

THE GENERAL PROPERTIES OF SYSTEM BOUNDARIES

How are we to distinguish between a political system and its setting? Does it make empirical as well as theoretic sense to say that a political system has a boundary dividing it from its environment? If so, how are we to define the line of demarcation?

The difficulties that beset us in seeking to answer these questions can be exposed, if not fully clarified, if we briefly consider other types of behaving or empirical systems with respect to which the existence of system boundaries is in much less doubt. By examining these systems and discovering the true significance of boundaries as a concept, we shall be in a better position to appreciate the utility and reality of attributing apparently similar boundaries to systems of social interaction, such as political systems.

The boundaries of physical and biological systems

All types of systems that have been found useful for research in the natural sciences are alike at least in that none of them functions in a vacuum in the phenomenal world. They are all imbedded in some kind of environment in fact, even though for heuristic purposes it may be necessary to exclude the influence of the setting temporarily, as in the case of the study of gravity under conditions of a frictionless world. Yet even though all systems are to be found in some kind of setting, they are able to maintain their identity with sufficient distinctiveness so that it is relatively easy for us to distinguish them from their environment.

From this perspective a boulder is one of the simplest of physical systems. Its density separates it from the surrounding air, and its parts share a common destiny as long as it retains its character as a boulder. Thereby we are able to distinguish it from adjacent boulders and the ground upon which it rests. The boundary between the boulder and other things is clear and unmistakable.

Our solar system, consisting of the sun and its satellites, similarly represents by its very designation a physical system of interest. Imaginatively and literally, given the technology, we could draw a line around it to designate its physical boundary. We can even consider the interaction of its parts as though, for the moment, it were not affected by the gravitational field of its own galaxy or even larger segments of the universe. Yet we know that the destiny of the solar system is irrevocably linked to the broader environment outside its spatial boundaries.

A waterfall as well may be considered a system of behavior, even though in this instance there is the complication that after a brief stay each drop of water constantly leaves the system never to appear again. This rapid flow of the water through the system does not lead us to confuse the waterfall with the precipice over which it cascades, the river feeding the water and drawing it away, or the winds contributing to its turbulence. Indeed, even though disturbances to the system may change the rate of flow of the water, the boundaries will usually change only marginally. They tend to be quite stable during short intervals of time.

An apple is an organic system isolated from its environment by a skin. We take it for granted that if our task is to understand the processes occurring within the apple itself as it matures and decays, we need to take into consideration factors outside of the skin itself. The soil in which the apple tree grows, the nature of the tree itself, and when parted from this, the humidity, temperature, and circulation of the atmosphere in which the apple is stored are all of decisive importance for the life of the apple as a system. Yet, from the point of view of the horticulturalist, these elements are variables external to the apple as an organic system. The boundary is well defined by the skin.

The human body is another biological system whose boundaries consist not of an imaginary line but of an epidermis that seems to mark it off unambiguously from its environment. In the maturation process we quickly learn not to confuse things bounded by our skin and those outside.

In each of these examples of physical or biological systems the boundaries seem simple enough to perceive. They form the spatial or material limits to the collection of variables in which we are interested. Either they in fact contain these variables, like an envelope, as the skin of an apple or of the human body, or it requires very little stretching of the imagination to conceive of some kind of shell surrounding them, as for the boulder, waterfall, or solar system. Such a container would decisively mark off the relevant variables from their surroundings.

But a system of social interactions, such as a political system, is normally so diffused throughout a society that we have considerable difficulty in accommodating the same imagery to these actions, taken collectively, that we apply so easily to physical and biological systems. A system of social interaction need not and usually does not include all of the actions of the person or group. Of course, if we were thinking of a specific political organization, such as a legislature, political party, interest group, or court, it is not beyond the bounds of our imagination to think of each of these organizations as possessing a physical boundary. At least we could think of scooping up all the members identified with these organizations and containing them within the walls of one building, if it could be built large enough.

We know that political interactions do not occur only within such well-defined goal-oriented structures. Much behavior occurs in other contexts, entirely outside a political organization, as in the illustrations mentioned earlier with regard to the family or an economic organization such as a bank. Furthermore, persons may act in political roles only intermittently, in the course of behaving economically or religiously, so that they may well seem to be popping in and out of a political system, as it were. We often talk politics at work, at social gatherings, and the like. When we take into account all kinds of political behavior, suffused as they are throughout society, it certainly seems to put a considerable strain on language as well as imagery to think of containing political interactions in some sort of envelope or within spatial boundary lines.

The general character of all boundaries

The circumscribing of boundaries for physical and biological systems seems to be simple enough. They do not seem to depend upon a decision on the part of the investigator but appear to be given in nature as though the systems were indeed purely natural in kind. But the simplicity in conceptualization of the boundaries is quite deceptive. These boundaries are, in fact, not phenomenally out there waiting to be identified. They conform to our general conclusion about the character of systems, that they are products of analytic selection; this is also true with regard to the boundaries of political systems.

We select the density of a boulder, the imaginary celestial line around our solar system, the form of the waterfall, and the skin of the apple and of the human being because we are particularly interested in understanding what happens to a set of variables defined by these limits. Although these are boundaries that we have become habituated to accepting, they stem from decisions that indicate the nature and limits of the theoretical or, for the layman, the practical interests on the part of the observer. If we had so wished, we could have ignored these boundaries and drawn entirely different ones. We could have considered each of these systems to be subsystems of a broader suprasystem consisting respectively of all rock formations constituting, say, the Pre-Cambrian shield, the Milky Way Galaxy, a river system, an orchard, and (with Patrick Geddes) the human biological organism as part of the ecological system. In fact, with regard to the human skin, as cytologists move in the opposite direction and reduce it to its component cells, at a given point of refinement in analysis they have difficulty in differentiating the epidermal cells from the surrounding air. The skin as an apparently natural boundary disappears.

In many cases, therefore, we may be able to draw a physical line to represent a boundary for a system, but this is an accidental although useful empirical property of some systems only. Conceptually a boundary is something quite different from its possible physical representation. A boundary line stands rather as a symbol or spatial embodiment of the criteria of inclusion–exclusion with respect to a system. It is a summary way of referring phenomenally to what we have included in or left out of a system. If, for systems in which space is a significant dimension, we can point to a line or a container, we know immediately that what is inside is part of the system and what is outside may belong to other systems.

For systems in which spatial location is not well defined or highly differentiated with regard to other systems and in which there may be considerable interlacing of behavior from different systems, we need other ways of describing or identifying the boundaries. Since the systems cannot be spatially and wholly separated from each other, the boundaries can be identified by the criteria in terms of which we can for each interaction determine whether it falls inside or outside the system. For the political system, as I have indicated, the test is whether the interactions are more or less directly related to the authoritative allocations of values for a society.

Accordingly, what we choose to put inside our system, to consider within its boundaries, will depend upon what we wish to examine in detail; for scientific purposes we also expect that these variables will show considerable interrelationship and coherence. What we leave outside, as part of its environment, will be those factors that we can accept as givens. They represent the independent variables or parameters of the system. In identifying them we thereby relieve ourselves of the need to go into detail about how they arise and what induces them to take the values that they do.

The external as compared to the internal or dependent variables may well have major consequences for the operation of the system. The fact that we consider them to be parameters of the system is not to be interpreted as indicating their irrelevance or lesser significance for understanding the functioning of the system. Their exclusion from the system for purposes of analysis says nothing at all about their contribution to the persistence or transformation of the system. All that it indicates is that the interrelationship of those elements or variables included in the system is what we wish to understand. They are the strictly political variables. We leave the explanation of variations in the parameters to others who are specialists in those areas. We need to know how the parameters vary, but we usually accept these variations as "givens" and seek to trace out their impact on the dependent internal or political variables.

Here we are fundamentally in no different a methodological position than those who study the physical or biological systems already mentioned. The gravitational forces of the universe compose part of the relevant environment of the solar system; large changes in these forces may destroy this system. In the analysis of the functioning of the solar system, however, it is quite satisfactory to assume these changes, to ignore their causes, and to confine our interest exclusively to the behavior of our solar system.

Similarly with regard to the human organism as a biological system, inadequate provision of nourishment can lead to its destruction. Yet in order to be able to cope with the unique range of problems that confront them as specialists, biologists are not called upon to become professional students of agriculture or of the system of distribution and exchange within a society.

We do not need to conclude from this generalized description of what is involved in the delineation of boundaries that, once established, they are eternally fixed. If it should turn out that owing to some mistaken interpretation or lack of insight, in order to improve our understanding of the political system we must include within it some element previously assigned to the environment, we are faced with no crisis. We simply redefine the system to meet our analytic needs. Each time that we enlarge our system we simultaneously shrink the environment. If this seems to introduce an element of indeterminacy into our conceptualization, I can only refer to our discussion of what we mean by a system. It is a device to help us to understand a defined and redefinable area of human behavior, not a strait jacket to imprison analysis permanently within a preconceived mold or model.

The deceptive character
of geographic boundaries

It might appear that I am overstating the case against the spatial delineation of a political system. After all, we do have maps of societies and the boundaries on these maps represent positive constraints on the behavior of persons in the society. Are these not the physical boundaries of a political system? They are often referred to as geopolitical boundaries.

On the surface it may seem plausible to utilize geographic boundaries as coincident with our analytic ones. In fact, these are not the kind of limits which I am speaking of here. Geopolitical boundaries have important and obvious consequences for a political system and to that extent form an important variable. They do help to define the claims to and acceptance of the jurisdiction of a particular set of authorities, but they stand as the politically defined boundaries for the whole society, not solely of the political system in that society. Geopolitical boundaries do not help us to differentiate those interactions *within* the society that are political from those that are economic, religious, educational, or the like. They tell us when a person moves from the jurisdictional claims of one set of authorities into those of another; they do not help us to understand when this person moves from an economic setting to a political one. The geopolitical boundaries circumscribe all interlaced social systems of the society, not any specific social system.

From this discussion we must conclude that, in their theoretical status, boundaries of systems need not always be spatial in nature. Analytically, the boundaries of all systems may be interpreted as the criteria of inclusion in or exclusion from the systems forming the focus of interest. The fact that empirically a system of political interaction cannot be contained, unmixed with other social systems, by a line drawn on a map or cannot symbolically be put within an envelope of some sort that separates it unmistakably from other systems of social interaction does not weaken the utility of the concept "boundaries" as an analytic tool. It just compels us to recognize that physical boundaries are only one way of empirically separating systems.

EMPIRICAL INDICATORS OF BOUNDARIES OF POLITICAL SYSTEMS

Although empirically there is no physical line across which we might step as we move from one system to another, experience, nevertheless, lends reality to the existence of a boundary between political and other systems in a society. Most societies provide some clues as to when we move from one system of behavior to another, although the absence of manifest telltales need not be conclusive proof that an exchange between systems has not taken place.

The most distinctive indications of such exchanges occur in societies with a high degree of structural differentiation, as in modernized social systems. In such societies there is usually a sharp demarcation of many political roles from other kinds of roles. Members of a society will have different expectations with regard to the way persons will behave in political as compared with religious or familial roles, for example. As we move from a strictly religious or family setting to a political one, we are expected to change our rules of behavior in some known degree. If we did not, we would be looked upon as odd or ignorant. In other words, in a structurally highly differentiated society regularized patterns of expectations with regard to how we act in different situations provides one empirical test of the existence of boundaries between systems. This is so clearly the case that in ordinary conversation we often speak of a person "stepping out" of his role, say, as a religious leader or scientist and undertaking to act as a political prophet or politician.

In many societies, though, the analytically distinguishable kinds of behavior may be empirically fused. In various traditional, nonliterate societies, for example, a few structures may perform all the major tasks. Through the kinship structure alone all of the activities necessary for the persistence of the society may be carried out, such as the production of goods and services, transmission of cultural norms, inculcation of motivations, and the making of binding allocations. Under these conditions the political system would be completely embedded in this major structure and its components. A chief might act not only as the political chief, but as the ceremonial leader, the main economic decision maker, and the ultimate head of the kinship unit in its familial aspects. And in practice he might perform these varied kinds of actions virtually simultaneously. That is to say, a person might act in any analytically differentiated role without changing his setting or empirical role.

Under conditions such as these, empirical indicators of the boundary between the political and other social systems would be considerably more obscure than in modern societies. Even here, the society is not entirely devoid of empirical clues corresponding to the analytically distinguished kinds of behavior. A meeting of the elders of the clan, a council of war, or the introduction of a wand of authority in a ritual, cue the participants to the change of setting or of activity. In that sense, these cues provide evidence that the boundary into the political system of the society has been crossed.

It has been suggested that the degree of differentiation of political systems from other social systems and therefore, we may add, the clarity of the boundary between them is signalized by the following properties: (1) the extent of distinction of political roles and activities from other roles and activities, or conversely the extent to which they are all imbedded in limited structures such as the family or kinship groups; (2) the extent to which occupants of political roles form a separate group in the society and possess a sense of internal solidarity and cohesion; (3) the extent to which political roles take the shape of a hierarchy which is distinguishable from other hierarchies based upon wealth, prestige, or other nonpolitical criteria; and (4) the extent to which the recruitment processes and criteria of selection differ for the occupants of political as contrasted with other roles.[2] If we used indicators such as these, it would be possible to rank societies on a continuum with regard to the sharpness of definition and empirical delineation of intersystem boundaries.

THE ENVIRONMENT OF POLITICAL SYSTEMS

The intrasocietal systems

Those aspects of a society that fall outside the boundaries of a political system can be generalized by stating that they consist of all the other subsystems of the society. They constitute the environment of the political sys-

[2] See Eisenstadt, *The Political Systems of Empires.*

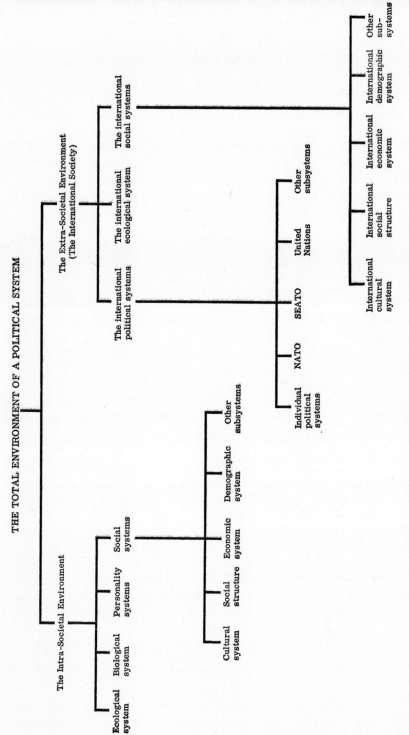

Table 1. Components of the Total Environment of a Political System.

tem. Environment embraces the social as well as the physical environment. Unless the context indicates otherwise, the concept will be used, henceforth, in both senses. But this universal environment, with its variety of differentiable systems, has two major aspects: that is, the numerous systems external to a political system are composed of two basically different types, intrasocietal and extrasocietal. Table 1 depicts this dichotomy and indicates the various kinds of systems that are included within each of these two major types.

Let us consider the classification scheme. By the environment we may be referring to that part of the social and physical environment that lies *outside* the boundaries of a political system and yet *within* the same society. This is the intrasocietal part of the environment. In examining the impact of the environmental changes on a political system, we would be referring to changes that occur in these other social systems. A depression in the economy, a change of values and aspirations in the culture, or a shift in the class structure may each have consequences for a political system. These changes occur in areas outside of what is normally conceived to be the political system; yet they take place within the same society as the one that contains the political system. This part of the total environment will engage a considerable share of our attention. When we move beyond it into the extrasocietal systems, we are in effect dealing with what we normally call the international political system.

This intrasocietal part of the environment of a political system may be classified in many ways, but it will be helpful to simplify and order it by dividing it into several systems. The following may be identified as some of the major external intrasocietal systems of importance to the persistence and change of political systems: the ecological, biological, personality, and social systems.

There is nothing predetermined or sacrosanct about this classification scheme. Alternative formulations could be easily visualized. Since the mode of analysis to be explored does not rest definitively on the specific categorization of the environment of the political system, we do not need to pause very long over it. The important point, rather, requires that we recognize the fact of the environment and the theoretical problems it occasions. Without this, we could not proceed to suggest a kind of analysis designed to shed light on the way in which political systems are able to persist and change or cope with the stresses to which they are constantly exposed.

To indicate what is involved in the major intrasocietal environmental systems, we shall examine each in turn, but only very briefly. The ecological system encompasses the physical environment and the nonhuman organic conditions of human existence. In the physical part of the ecological system may be included geographical or spatial characteristics such as the nature of the physical resources, topography, size of territory, climate, and similar properties that influence the conditions of all existence including the political. The nonhuman organic aspects of the environmental systems refer to the nature, location, and accessibility of food supply and other flora and fauna that can be utilized by members of a political system. Variations in food supply, both for nomadic and sedentary societies, are known to affect the structure and processes of political systems, if technology is accepted as a constant.[3]

The biological system in the environment draws attention to the fact that in seeking to understand political processes, it is easy to neglect the hereditary properties that may help to determine human motivation in political as well as other social contexts. It refers to that aspect of political interactions that is determined or influenced by the biological make-up of human beings. To the extent that genetic characteristics impose limits upon the behavior of individuals, this may have implications for political life. Capacities for pacific or rational behavior, for cooperation as compared to conflict, are said to be related to the genetic inheritance of human beings. Orthodox Freudians have insisted on the inherent aggressive drives which all social arrangements, including the political, can ignore only at their peril.[4] The validity of this proposition is not at stake here; rather the only point is that politically relevant biological traits cannot be neglected as part of the total environment in which a political system operates. The fact that political science tends to do so, does not, of course, reduce either their theoretical or empirical importance.

Personality and social systems have received the widest and most detailed attention in the traditional literature. Social systems may be classified into several types: cultural, social structural, economic, and demographic. Here again the precise subdivision is not crucial.

Variations in the nature of the personalities and acquired motivations of members of a political system have long drawn the attention of students of politics. The science of ethology toward which John Stuart Mill was reaching and recent efforts around the theme of national character and variable kinds of political behavior presumed to be associated with different types of

---

[3] E. R. Leach, *Political Systems of Highland Burma* (Cambridge: Harvard University Press, 1954), in which political structure seems to shift with movement from plains to hill agriculture; Schapera, *Government and Politics in Tribal Societies*, especially Chaps. I and VI and p. 219.

[4] See S. Freud, *Group Psychology and the Analysis of the Ego* (New York: Liveright Publishing Corp., 1951) and *Civilization and Its Discontents* (New York: Doubleday & Company, Inc., 1958); E. F. M. Durbin and J. Bowlby, *Personal Aggressiveness and War* (New York: Columbia University Press, 1939), and the same authors with others, *War and Democracy* (London: Routledge & Kegan Paul, Ltd., 1938).

personalities reflect a firm recognition of the role of this major parameter.[5]

Fluctuations in the social culture by which personalities are shaped and in the economy, shifts in the general structure of society or in specific aspects of it (as in the number and size of group formations or of social classes) and changes in the size, rate of growth, composition, and distribution of populations are known to have high significance for what happens in the relevant political system. A great deal of the effort of political research has gone into seeking to trace out, informally at least, the relationships between the political system and these environmental or parametric systems. Although I shall not interpret it as the task of an introduction to systems analysis to seek to extract systematically the actual relationships that exist between any of these parametric systems and the political system, nevertheless, a major effort will be directed toward devising a satisfactory set of categories for doing so.

Extrasocietal systems

The systems just identified are part of the same society of which the political system itself is a social subsystem. In this sense, these systems are external to the political system. Any influence they exert on the political system must derive from the fact that actions bridge the boundary between one or another of them and of the political system. This is the first sense in which a system may be said to be external to or in the environment of a political system.

But a system is external to a political system in a second and different sense. It may lie outside the society of which the political system itself is a social subsystem; yet it may have important consequences for the persistence or change of a political system. Instances of this are societies and political systems that are different from the society and political system under consideration. From the point of view of the United States, France is a society

---

[5] See N. J. Smelser and W. T. Smelser, eds., *Personality and Social Systems* (New York: John Wiley & Sons, Inc., 1963); J. S. Mill, *A System of Logic,* Book VI, especially Chap. V which is significantly entitled "Of Ethology, of the Science of the Formation of Character"; L. W. Pye, *Politics, Personality and Nation Building* (New Haven: Yale University Press, 1962); Lipset and Lowenthal, *Culture and Social Character;* R. E. Lane, *Political Life* (New York: Free Press of Glencoe, Inc., 1959), especially Part III and the many references found there, and *Political Ideology* (New York: Free Press of Glencoe, Inc., 1962) especially p. 400 ff.; A. Inkeles and D. J. Levinson, "National Character: The Study of Modal Personality and Sociocultural Systems," in *Handbook of Social Psychology,* G. Lindzey, ed. (Cambridge, Mass.: Addison-Wesley, 1954), II, 977-1020, and an extensive bibliography therein; D. Tomašić, *Personality and Culture in Eastern European Politics* (New York: George W. Stewart, Publisher, Inc., 1948); F. L. K. Hsu, ed., *Psychological Anthropology: Approaches to Culture and Personality* (Homewood, Ill.: The Dorsey Press, Inc., 1961), especially the essay by A. Inkeles, "National Character and Modern Political Systems," pp. 172-207.

and contains a political system the consequences of the actions of which may cross the boundary of the American political system and help to shape its destinies.

We can broaden considerably this image of the external environment if we also view the whole international society as a unit external to any given political system. We may consider it a vital part of the extrasocietal environment. In fact, it is a summary way of referring to the whole of this environment, including the individual societies as subsystems of the international society. From this point of view, as components of the international society, we would find an international ecological system, an international political system, and such international social systems as an international culture, an international economy, an international demographic system, and so forth, just as in the case of the domestic societies. The international society as a whole or any of its subsystems would constitute parameters in the extrasocietal environment of a given political system and would have to be taken into account as possible sources of influence upon what happens within the given system. Among the international subsystems would also be found various collections of political subsystems such as NATO, SEATO, the United Nations, or the Soviet bloc, and each of these might have separate effects on a given political system.

The task will be to devise a conceptual structure for systematically and economically tracing out the exchanges of the extra- and intrasocietal parameters with a given political system. Diagram 1 provides a highly and inexpressibly oversimplified version of the relationships just discussed. It is presented here as another way of interpreting the classification shown in Table 1 and offers a simple spatial representation of the exchanges between a system and the various components of its environment. At a later point I shall be able to modify this diagram so as to show, first, the dynamic relationship of a political system to its environment and, second, the flow of the influences of the environment through the system.

In reply to the questions with which we began this discussion, we have seen that political life may be described as a set or system of interactions defined by the fact that they are more or less directly related to the authoritative allocation of values for a society. Although similar allocations occur within other organizations, I shall find it useful to include within our range of theoretical concern only societal political systems rather than parapolitical systems. However, much of our conceptual structure might apply equally well, with the necessary modifications, to the parapolitical systems of organizations.

What happens to a political system, its stability or change, will in part be a function of the operations of internal variables, the elements we are primarily concerned with understanding and explaining. The way in which they function, the stresses imposed upon them, and the behavior that occurs as a response to such stress will also be a product of what takes place in the total environment of the political system. A political system is an open one

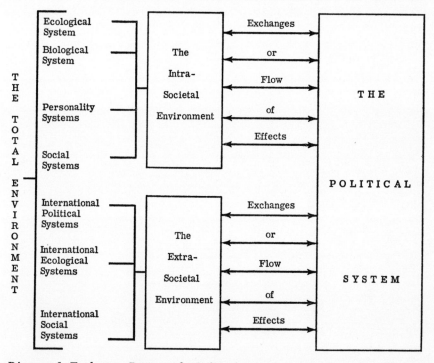

Diagram 1. Exchanges Between the Political System and the Total Environment

in the sense that it is exposed, in varying degrees, to the events that occur in its environment. The concepts "boundary" and "environment" help to order our analysis with these desiderata in mind. A major effort with which we shall shortly be confronted will be to devise a further set of concepts adequate for simplifying and systematizing the study of the *relationships* between a system and its total environment.

Before proceeding to this task, we require additional preparation. I have specified the nature of a system as such, identified the characteristics of the system I shall be calling political, and called attention to the easily neglected setting in which this system must exist. This puts us in a position to open the door fully to the kind of theoretical analysis that becomes possible now that we have taken these first small steps. In the process of doing so we shall be able to explore additional significant properties of the political system as a system of behavior.

SIX

Persistence in a World of Stability and Change

A systems theoretic approach, as indicated in the preceding chapters, may share with other kinds of analyses the conception that its subject matter is a system imbedded in an environment and exposed to what happens there. In other words, it is an open system. In this and the succeeding chapter we shall discover that what distinguishes the systems theory being developed here is that it presents a view of political life as a responding system as well. It constitutes a set of behaviors through which positive action may be taken to cope with the influences operating on it.

SYSTEM PERSISTENCE

The peculiar characteristic that political systems share with other social systems, and even some mechanical and biological ones, is that they are not necessarily defenseless in the face of disturbances to which they may be subjected. The processes and structures of political systems are not freely buffeted about by the vagaries of chance. Because of the kind of system it is, the members of a political system have the opportunity, of which, however, they may not always take advantage, to respond to stress in such a way as to try to assure the persistence of some kind of system for making and executing binding decisions.

It is the identification of this phenomenon—that political systems through their own responding actions are capable of persisting even in a world of rapid change—that poses a central question for theoretical inquiry. Just as natural science seeks to understand the fundamental processes underlying organic life, I shall propose that it is the task of a behavioral science of politics to put kinds of questions that reveal the way in which the life processes or defining functions of political systems are protected. Regardless of time or place, what makes it possible for a system to assure the perpetuation of any means through which values may be authoritatively allocated, that is, to permit the system to persist? How is any political system able to cope with the stresses that may threaten to destroy it so that even when critically undermined by such extraordinary events as civil wars, revolutions, or military defeat a system of some sort may manage to rise again?

This is not just a matter of whether a given type of political system is able to cope with its problems and manages to survive; or being unable to handle them, succumbs and is transformed into a new type of system. A broader question draws our attention: How is it that in the face of continuing blows, from within or without, even the minimal organization, cooperation, commitment of resources and energies, and obedience to authority are possible? Without these conditions binding decisions could not be formulated or put into effect, and no political life could endure, regardless of the particular structure or form the system might take.

For purposes of what we might call an allocative type of theory (the form of theory implicit in traditional political research) as against a system-coping and persistence kind of theory, we would be predisposed to ask other kinds of questions. How do political systems operate? How do they in fact allocate values? What are the forces determining the nature and outcomes of the various processes and structures through which authoritative allocations are formulated and put into effect?

For systems analysis, however, certain key problems logically come before these. They concern the conditions under which such allocative processes and structures themselves may persist. These are the life processes of any and all systems.

At the theoretical level, for example, it is as though from an interest in personality systems we were to set aside inquiry into specific personality types and the behavior of individuals characterized by such types. Our main task would be to probe into the general processes, common to all personality structures, through which threats imposed upon the integrity of the system might be handled. In a comparable way, systems analysis impels us to direct our attention to the very life processes of political systems rather than to the specific structures or processes that make a particular kind of regime viable. Initially and as a point of departure, it turns our interest away from comparing different types of political systems. Rather, systems analysis directs our attention toward the processes that all types of political systems share and that make it possible for them to cope, however successfully, with stresses that threaten to destroy the capacity of a society to sustain any political system at all.

Although it is necessary to pose such questions as these in order to obtain the proper focus on the development of a conceptual structure for the analysis of political systems, it would go beyond the limits of this volume to attempt to answer them fully here. But it is vital to realize the significance of such questions if we are to be able to formulate an appropriate preliminary approach for an understanding of the political system. They suggest that if we are ultimately to understand the way in which a system persists over time, we must begin by addressing ourselves to a number of issues that will help to clarify the meaning of persistence, stress, and responses to it.

It will lead to such questions as: What are the sources of stress? What is meant by the concept "persistence"? What do we mean when we say that stress threatens such persistence? What concepts do we need if we are to study the way in which stress is brought to bear on political systems? When we have finished discussing these questions, our inquiry into the indispensable conceptual foundation that underlies a systems analysis of political life will have been brought to a close.

GENERAL SOURCES OF STRESS

The sources of stress need not always be quite so dramatic as wars, revolutions, or other social traumas. Indeed, normally they are much more prosaic. They are just as likely to stem from the constant, daily pressures of political life. Without any aid from special crises, they seem capable of imposing serious strains on the ability of any political system to survive or on the ability of the members of a society to assure any arrangement for making and implementing authoritative decisions. On the face of it, it is little short of miraculous that the basic political functions are met in some way, so great are the internal strains to which any system is typically and normally subjected and so overpowering the external changes that they frequently must be capable of absorbing.

Internal sources

What are the sources of this stress upon the capacity of a system to endure? The meaning of stress will be reconsidered later in this chapter.

Temporarily, we can accept any intuitive understanding of it. As normally defined, stress may come from two directions, the one internal and the other external; external here will mean stress from the intrasocietal and extra-societal environment.

If we look first at the possible recurring internal sources of strain, disorganization, or destruction, we can see that by virtue of the very kinds of substantive matters political systems are called upon to deal with, the relationships among the members of a system tend to become the focus of the sharpest forms of antagonism in society. Scarcity is perhaps the most significant phenomenon of all societies, not always in any absolute sense but in light of the expectations of the members of the society. In every society there is a variety of means for regulating or resolving differences with regard to the way in which scarce values are to be distributed and used. But where such differences cannot be adjusted privately, that is, autonomously, among the members of the society or where the achievement of a goal requires mobilization of the resources and energies of all members of a system, resort to some sort of political allocation becomes inevitable.

The significance of control over political instrumentalities—even if it means just having the strongest voice in the meeting of elders in a band of Bushmen—has never been lost to men in any society, however small and simple. Control over these means has seldom been left to mere chance; it has usually been a matter of the gravest concern and strife. From the smallest and simplest traditional societies to the largest and most complex modern ones, there have been at least a few who have been willing, even eager, to risk the deepest conflicts so that they might have an effective voice in establishing the basic political arrangements or the particular objectives and goals within an already existing structure.

Yet, in the face of the strains occasioned through the passions so aroused, surprisingly few societies have succumbed because of their inability to provide some kind of structures and processes for the authoritative allocation of values. The destruction of political systems exposed to such constant tension among its members might well have been expected to occur with considerable frequency. The ability of some kind of political system to endure in a society might be something to gaze at with wonder had we not come to take it so much for granted as the normal course of things.

External sources

For those systems that escape or are spared the ravages of internal conflict, it is even more remarkable that, in recent times especially, they have not foundered on the sharper and more dangerous shoals located in the total environment of the system. Industrialization and everything it drags in its train have become the most potent recent source of change. Political systems in societies that had previously been changing slowly, in some cases so slowly that few differences were readily perceptible between many generations, have with apparent suddenness been exposed to forces that have enormously speeded up the rate of change. The nature and range of problems that have now been thrust upon these political systems have altered radically. Political systems in process of organization are confronted with the breakdown of fundamental order or the task of seeking to achieve unity in the face of conflicting internal loyalties. The so-called revolution of rising expectations, the need to provide for self-defense with limited economic resources, newly discovered lateral and vertical mobility within hitherto relatively impermeable social structures, resistant tribalism and other pluralist groups, difficult options in the area of international relations, all combine to impose severe external strains on the members of newly emerging political systems.

These are, in significant part, products of industrialism as it acts on rural, peasant, and nonliterate traditional systems. But where industrialism is well entrenched, the second Industrial Revolution of the mid-twentieth century has generated its own special problems related to the rate of economic change and the capacity of societies to devise political policies and structures to cope with it.

Historically, in almost every instance where vast economic and social changes have occurred, the political system has also been transformed, often into almost unrecognizable new entities. But as with internal sources of stress, these external ones have in only exceptional instances left a society incapable of settling upon some form of political system, a condition, which, if it occurred, would bring the whole society toppling down with it. The structure of political life may change. Its goals may be basically and permanently revised. The personnel may be new and inexperienced, and the substantive decisions it arrives at may be discontinuous with the past. So seldom are societies incapable of establishing some regularized procedures and structures for authoritatively allocating values that we take it for granted that even in the face of the most violent upheavals, ultimately some type of political system will emerge.

Conflict in a political system generated by environmental influences usually concerns such problems as the type of system, the personnel who are to hold positions of authority, or the policies they ought to pursue. These are vital enough. But seldom is there at stake the survival of any political system at all. On occasion, a Congo may be set loose to fend for itself without adequate preparations for an overarching political order. A Walter Bagehot may read into the political turmoil accompanying the demise of the Second Republic in France the threat of utter chaos through the irremediable collapse of all political organization.[1] But only in exceptional cases do these moments in history end in the destruction and termination of a society for want of a system through which binding decisions may be effectuated.

THE MEANING OF PERSISTENCE

In the face of stress through disturbances and changes such as these, if we had to rely purely on conjecture, we might well have concluded otherwise and predicted that political systems could only have a very brief life span. Yet it is clear that many have persisted through time, perhaps quantitatively not so many as have succumbed or been absorbed by others. It does pose the problem of how some have managed to persist while others have disappeared. To answer this question, we shall be led to consider the fundamental life processes of political systems. Before doing so, we are confronted with the task of clarifying what we mean by the term "persistence" itself.

The disappearance or nonpersistence of systems

When we say that a system has persisted over time, what is to be conveyed by this expression? It will help point up the answer if we first look at what is meant by the antithesis: When can we say that a system has, in fact, failed to persist?

To say that a system has failed may mean one of two things: that it has changed but continues to exist in some form; or that it has disappeared entirely. As the first meaning indicates, a system can be said to persist even if it changes. At first glance this may seem rather paradoxical. We can, however, set this puzzling proposition aside for the moment. At the very least it helps us to understand what is meant by persistence if we interpret its negative to mean, in its second sense, that a system has disappeared completely. For the given society authoritative allocations of values could no longer be made.

This outcome is neither impossible nor unusual. It has occurred when the membership of a society has been utterly destroyed through some natural catastrophe such as an earthquake or epidemic, or when the society has failed to reproduce itself biologically, as perhaps in the case of the Mesa Verde Indians. It may happen in the limiting case when, for whatever reason, a war of all against all, in the Hobbesian sense, breaks out and cooperation becomes impossible even for the minimal purposes of law and order.

[1] Mrs. R. Barrington, *Works and Life of Walter Bagehot* (London: Longmans, Green & Co., Inc., 1915), Vol. I, the seven "Letters on the French Coup d'État."

Upon receipt of its nominal independence in 1960, the Belgian Congo approached as closely to this limit as any society in the twentieth century. For some period it was doubtful that any set of authorities would ever be able to speak and act for the whole society or command the allegiance of most members. The Congo was on the verge of disintegrating into a multitude of lesser political systems co-extensive with tribal groups or some of the former Belgian administrative districts.

Political systems have also disappeared at moments of social catastrophe when, as the result of civil war, revolution or military defeat, the previously existing political unit has collapsed to be replaced temporarily by independent, law-abiding centers, or lawless bands. Germany, momentarily, at the end of World War II, France during periods of the French Revolution, Russia during the height of the Revolution, and (in anticipation) forecasts of probable conditions in any major political system after the first few days of atomic warfare[2] illustrate this state of affairs. Historical political systems have disappeared, some permanently, others to recover their integrity, at the hands of conquerors, when they have been absorbed into alien systems. The political systems of the American Indian, of Scotland, or of the Baltic societies are examples of these types.

Hence, it appears that nonpersistence points to a condition that involves more than mere change. It suggests the complete breakdown and evaporation of a political system.

Absolutely stable systems

Let us look at the polar extreme of utter disappearance and construe persistence to mean, perhaps, that a system continues without any change at all, in a state of complete stability. If we sought such a system, we would find it only where a political system has remained intact over a specified interval of time. Such a system might occur under two conditions. First, it might appear if the environment itself showed no changes. In the short run this might well be possible but certainly not in the long run. Empirically we can point to no system in which the environment has remained perfectly unchanged. Even the relatively static traditional and tribal systems of yesterday are today undergoing profound alteration due to shifts in such parameters as culture and economy.

Second, a system might remain intact if it could shelter itself from every disturbance in its environment as well as from internally generated pressures on its structures and processes. Either the patterns of behavior constituting the political system would have to be impervious to change, or

[2] See *Human Organization,* 16 (1957) for a special issue devoted to the problems of "Human Adaptation to Disaster" together with an extensive bibliography.

members of the system would have to be able to handle change in such a way as to ward off their effects, which amounts to the same thing.

It is true that to some extent every system has the ability to insulate itself, at least in part, from both extrasocietal and intrasocietal disturbances in the environment. However, no system has yet succeeded in doing so permanently or fully. For limited periods of time this has been attempted with varying measures of success and with regard to limited parameters. Switzerland has been able to avoid becoming entangled in military conflicts and international political alliances for centuries, with a few exceptions during the periods of the French Revolution and the League of Nations. For two centuries Japan was able to ward off contact with the West and, thereby, at least the effects of the Industrial Revolution as well.

Systems have been able to shelter themselves not only from changes in such extrasocietal forces, but also from those of some intrasocietal parameters. In the last two decades the wide amplitude of fluctuations in the business cycle, with their attendant political repercussions, have been reduced with some tentative measure of success, at least in Western industrialized societies.

However, it is clear that if immurement of a political system is effective at all, it endures for only limited periods of time or with respect to restricted aspects of external disturbances. No system can be expected to escape all of the ravages of internal or external change. We could scarcely interpret persistence to mean the maintenance of a system free from any changes at all. Certainly in the long run, significant differences appear in what may be identified as continuing political systems.

Persistence with and through change

This approach introduces something of a paradox. Persistence implies something less than a perfectly static condition; it is not incompatible with change. Indeed, in most cases, even in the not-so-long run, if a system is to persist, it must be able to change or adapt itself to fluctuating circumstances. It cannot expect to be able to fend off all disturbances.

Not even so stable a system as that of the United States can be described as having remained unchanged over the years, even if we discount entirely the effect of formal amendments to the Constitution. Through changing practices and through decisions of the Supreme Court during the Roosevelt period of the thirties the federal system was radically transformed. Yet certainly a political system has managed to persist in the United States over the years. Similarly in Germany, although the imperial order fell to the Weimar Republic which in turn yielded to the Nazi regime to be succeeded by a third order after World War II, some form of political system persisted. Change does not seem to be incompatible with continuity. It seems possible and necessary to say that a system endures if, at the same time, it undergoes substantial and significant alterations.

To take a further illustration, the British political system has certainly not stood still over the centuries. It has been radically modified in a number of ways. But through it all, the system has maintained its basic identity as a system continuing through time. In geographic scope the original English political community (the continuing core over the centuries) has expanded to include Scotland and northern Ireland, and at one time it embraced the whole of a now shrunken empire. Neither have the characteristics of the British regime remained constant and intact. Historically it has shown wide fluctuations, ranging from a variety of political systems under competing Anglo-Saxon warlords to the beginning of centralization in the Tudor monarchs. A semipopular dictatorship under Cromwell, a constitutional and partly representative monarchical political order during the eighteenth and nineteenth centuries, and a broadening popular democracy during the late nineteenth and the twentieth centuries succeeded each other in turn. In the process the Cabinet system of government with responsible parties and an all but completely atrophied royal prerogative took shape.

It is clear that fundamental transformations have taken place in the original form of the British political system, however we may identify it, with respect to which the present political system can weave a material and historical connection. It would certainly be stretching the point beyond reason and conviction to argue that the present British political system represents a continuation of the original miscellaneous Celtic political systems or even less numerous Anglo-Saxon ones. Nevertheless, it is quite meaningful and useful to interpret the history of English political life in terms of the persistence of some way of making authoritative allocations of values.

It shows continuity in two senses. In the first, the present members of the British political system possess a feeling and belief in their historical identity with earlier political systems. It is a strongly held belief that is capable of stirring members to action. This traditional ideological element helps to maintain a current sense of mutual identification, and this represents a component of the input of support for a political system.

In the second sense, there is genuine material continuity with respect to a political community whose membership has changed. At each historical point we can describe the kind of transformations or alterations in the then existing system which made possible the continuance of a pattern of relationships through which binding decisions could be made and implemented. At this general level a political system of some sort has persisted through time with respect to the British society, even though this society itself has changed its character and extent. Over the ages the life processes of a political system have somehow been sustained; there has always been a set of institutions and practices through which all of the basic political functions could be fulfilled.

What has been said by way of illustration about the British political system could be duplicated for any particular currently existing political system, insofar as it has managed to adapt in some way over time and can trace some historical connection with a set of pre-existing political systems. In this sense, it is much more plausible to state that a system may endure even if at the same time it undergoes substantial and significant changes in some of its aspects.

PERSISTENCE AND THE LEVEL OF ANALYSIS

The point being made here is that whether or not we consider a political system as persisting will depend upon the level at which we examine it. If we consider its authorities, certainly they may change very frequently; similarly its regime or the scope of its community may vary. If we go beyond these to the most general level of a system, namely, to that at which we would be concerned only with the existence of some ways for making authoritative allocations—what we may call the fundamental life processes of a political system—persistence in the presence of change at other levels becomes quite plausible.

For the mode of analysis under construction, the critical level to which our inquiry is directed is not that of the particular form or type of system. We will not be concerned with what is undoubtedly one kind of vital question: What are the stresses on a given type of political system such as a democracy or totalitarian one? How do one or the other of these systems manage to survive or become transformed into something different? For systems analysis, this is a second order kind of problem, however critical and urgent it may be with respect to the on-going policies of a system or immediate needs.

The first order problem concerns the way in which the fundamental functions necessary for systems persistence and which are expressed through specific types of processes and structures, are safeguarded in a society. Given the various kinds of stress that might have made it unlikely for any political system to endure, we need to become interested in the way in which the members of political systems have managed to handle these stresses so that, at a minimum, some kind of authoritative processes for allocating values could be assured.

Persistence and change

Persistence or survival by virtue of change is thus not so puzzling as it has appeared on the surface. By it no more is meant than that if, in any society, a system for fulfilling the basic political function of making and executing binding allocations is to continue, the members must be prepared to cope with disturbances, whatever their origin, that lead to stress. If necessary, they may even be compelled to modify the system in one or another of its major aspects. The only exception occurs where the intra- or extrasocietal changes have no effect on the system, as when members of a system actively seek to bring this condition about by sealing the system off from possible disturbances. Otherwise, the members of a system may have to give up part of their membership, for example, in military conquest where the terms of surrender require the cession of territory. If deep internal differences have developed over the proper goals for which the members of the system are to strive collectively or over the structure of organization through which they are to be achieved, they may be led to recast the regime. Alternatively, members of a system may find it necessary to change, not its long-range goals that I would include as part of the regime, but its shorter-range policies through the acceptance of varying sets of political authorities, as in the case of democracies.

What this signifies, therefore, is that the cost of survival of some means for dealing with otherwise unresolved differences in a society may at times require the acceptance of change in one or all of the significant aspects of a political system, depending upon the circumstances. The members must be capable of modifying their political system, as circumstances dictate, with respect to its scope, membership, structure and processes, goals, or rules of behavior; or they must be able to manipulate their environment so as to relieve the stress. Only where in some way they can entirely fend off the effects of environmental change or where change is negligible, might we expect a system to persist even though it were not endowed with this capacity to adapt through self-transformation or manipulation of the environment. Otherwise, persistence of patterns of interaction capable of meeting the fundamental political functions requires that the members engaging in this activity be able to adapt, correct, readjust, control, or modify the system or its parameters to cope with the problems created by internal or external stress.

We can expect that variable means will be at hand for this purpose, limited only by such constraints as are imposed by resources, traditions, the ingenuity of members in the face of novel situations, and their available skills. Self-regulation by the members of a political system, even to the point of self-transformation in structure and goals, represents critical capabilities of all social systems.[3] Without them, a political system would be left to drift helplessly in the winds of change.

[3] Deutsch, *The Nerves of Government,* Chaps. 11-13.

Persistence versus *self-maintenance*

It is the fact that persistence may include the idea of change that makes it vital and necessary to differentiate this concept from that of systems maintenance. My analysis is not directed to seeking to explore the latter problem alone, or primarily. It is one matter to inquire into the conditions through which a system is able to maintain itself and quite another to seek to reveal the conditions of persistence.

Maintenance is weighted with the notion of salvaging the existing pattern of relationships and directs attention to their preservation. Persistence signalizes the importance of considering, not any particular structure or pattern, but rather the very life processes of a system themselves. In this sense a system may persist even though everything else associated with it changes continuously and radically. The idea of systems persistence extends far beyond that of systems maintenance; it is oriented toward exploring change as well as stability, both of which may be interpreted as alternative avenues for coping with stress.

If we wished, we could adopt the concept "maintenance" to apply to the life processes themselves. Fundamentally no theoretical harm would be done, as long as we imputed the required meaning to it. But the need to distinguish sharply the maintenance of a particular kind of system, or set of structure and political processes, from the perpetuation of the basic functions of political life—what I shall later describe as the essential variables of a political system—compels us to adopt a different concept. Maintenance is too heavily charged with the idea of stability and, as normally used, quite alien to the idea of change. Hence, systems analysis delves into a theory that explains the capacities of a system to persist, not to maintain itself as this would be normally understood. It seeks a theory of persistence, not of self-maintenance or equilibrium.

The thrust of systems analysis away from systems maintenance as a central organizing theme is felt in another way. Even though systems analysis recognizes that the members of political systems have the capacity to seek to cope with stress and change, this does not mean that all systems must behave adaptively or are equally successful in doing so. There need be no eufunctional[4] or maintenance-satisfying bias to this kind of analysis. Some systems may be equipped to deal only with relatively harmonious internal relations and constant external ones. This seems to have been true of the Fox Indians in North America who stressed harmony as against efficiency and success;[5]

[4] For this term see Levy, Jr., *Structure of Society*, p. 77.
[5] W. B. Miller, "Two Concepts of Authority," *American Anthropologist*, 57 (1955), 271-89.

even if they had remained independent, they would have encountered severe difficulties in coping with European culture.

Others may be better suited to deal with change. For example, structurally highly differentiated political systems have specialized organs of adaptation in the form of well-defined political elites whose livelihood is assured through patrimonial or prebendary means or through taxation. Such an elite is thereby freed to devote itself exclusively to political tasks and to give the system the attention it may require. Where change comes to be expected and where it is nonetheless essentially unpredictable, as in modernized societies, such a degree of specialization of attention is crucial. Traditions are no longer a guide of how to meet changing situations. Other differentiated political structures, such as parties, provide some of the instrumentalities for effective action. They enable the elite to mobilize human and material resources and to commit them for the various purposes required by the new conditions. Specialized administrative staffs and the like help in the same objectives.[6]

Variable means toward persistence

This does not imply that the actual transformations that do occur must necessarily be the only type that might have made it likely for a system to endure. There will always remain the great "ifs" of history. Although the German political system shifted from the Weimar Republic to a totalitarian regime and in this way adapted to the stresses attendant upon defeat in World War I and its ensuing economic inflation, a considerable range of alternatives was possible. Variable policies, structures, and innovations are available and may be equally successful in assuring the persistence of *some* pattern of authoritative allocations. The particular path adopted is a function of more than the capacity of the members of a system to cope with change. My approach to the analysis of political systems will not help us to understand why any specific policies are adopted by the politically relevant members in a system. Furthermore, the capacity to adapt does not thereby dictate that any specific, successful way of doing so is morally better or worse than any other even if, under the circumstances, someone might prove that it was a necessary and, therefore, inescapable condition of persistence.

Rather, with respect to whatever actions that may happen to be taken, systems analysis is designed to clarify the consequences pertaining to the continued survival of *some* form of political life. In this sense, we are operating at the most elemental level of analysis. We are seeking to under-

---

[6] D. Apter, "Modernization in Ghana and Uganda," manuscript, n. d.; and see also, *The Political Kingdom in Uganda* (Princeton, N.J.: Princeton University Press, 1961) Chaps. 14 ff.

stand how it is possible for the basic political function of a society—its authoritative allocations of values—to be fulfilled, regardless of time and place.

STRESS ON A SYSTEM

We can further improve our grasp of the meaning of persistence and its implications for our mode of analysis if we consider what is involved in the idea of stress, those conditions that challenge the capacity of a system to persist. I have been suggesting that it is the results of the operation of stress and the inability of a system to cope with it that lead a system to collapse. A system will be able to persist if its members are able to undertake adequate action in the face of stress. By understanding the general conditions that are created when stress occurs or that we may identify as stressful, we shall be able to reveal the full implications of persistence as a central concept in systems analysis.[7]

Disturbance as the cause of stress

How do we know when a system is operating under stress? To be able to answer this question, two preliminary remarks are necessary. In the first place, stress may have occurred, in which case it would not be difficult to document. But the kind of stressful condition that will be of primary interest for us is that which is potential. It represents a threat to a system, endangering its capacity to survive but not necessarily destroying the system. It offers the members of a system a chance to regulate or eliminate the stressing conditions or to shield the system from them. Whether or not the potential is actualized to the detriment of the system will depend upon the ability of the members of the system to deal with the conditions creating the stress.

In the second place, stress may imply a change from a prior condition of some sort that was hospitable to the persistence of a system. This is not to be understood, however, as suggesting that every internal or environmental change will necessarily be stressful. From the point of view of the survival probabilities of a system, changes will range from insignificant to those that are either highly beneficial or damaging.

In order to identify those events or occurrences within a system or its environment that in some way can be expected to bring about, or have brought about, a change in the way a system operates, we may reserve for them the concept *disturbance*. Disturbances will refer to all activities in the

[7] In this volume the discussion on stress will be confined to those conditions that define stress. The specific circumstances that promote stress will not be investigated.

environment or within a system that can be expected to or do displace a system from its current pattern of operations, regardless of whether or not it is stressful for the system.

Disturbances will vary enormously both in numbers and variety. They will also vary with respect to their consequences; hence, they may be classified as neutral, benign, or stressful according to the degree to which they affect the chances for some or any kind of political system to persist. In some cases an activity may take place that simply makes no difference to the operations of a political system; or the effects are so slight as to be negligible. In other instances the disturbance may be of such a nature as to enhance the chances of the system for surviving as some kind of system. The discovery in the economic sector of society of new material resources or the invention of new technologies that markedly improve the general standard of living may so contribute to the satisfactions with the system as to reinforce existing support for it. The disturbances with which we shall be particularly preoccupied are those that threaten to prevent a system from functioning and that can, therefore, be designated as stressful.

Threaten or endanger are the key words. If allowed to run its course, a disturbance might lead to the complete destruction of the system and even prevent its continuity through resurrection in any other form. But if a system survives, *ipso facto* it must have been able to abort such a tendency. Then the disturbance presented a threat rather than an accomplished fact; it stressed the system without destroying it. Most of the kinds of stress we shall be analyzing are of this sort.

Stress as variation from the normal range of operation

At the outset it is necessary to recognize that the precise identification of a stressful condition in a system raises major problems, some of which are not amenable to solution, given the level of data and understanding we presently have about political life. Since the task of theory is to extend the frontiers of knowledge and not simply to codify what we already know, this handicap in itself need not deter us.

We can appreciate the plausibility of stress as a useful concept if we are willing to recognize that, as an idea, it at least makes intuitive good sense. This is a sufficient, if not always necessary, starting point in seeking to ascribe a more technical meaning to a term. In a loose but meaningful way, we are prone to talk of political systems undergoing stress. In doing so we generally have in mind conditions that may lead to the destruction and transformation of a system. Much has been written of democracy in crisis, the horse and buggy political structures in an age of streamlined jets, the inability of tribal political systems to withstand the impact of colonizing cultures, the dangers of democracy inherent in the cleavages associated with pluralistic societies, or the threats posed to authoritarian and totalitarian systems by fissures in their elites.

In characterizing systems in this way, whether or not we are conscious of it, we seem to be implying that for the specific types of system under consideration there is some *normal* pattern of operation which has been displaced. But if we were asked to spell out the normal level of operation that is thus being modified, we might have considerable difficulty in providing a measure that would be generally accepted. For example, what is the normal range of operation of a totalitarian system such as the Soviet Union? Would the entrenchment of an orderly and peaceful pattern of leadership succession stress the system enough so as to push it beyond its normal range with the result that it could no longer be considered totalitarian? Has the French democratic system disappeared under the stress of the Gaullist regime or does it continue to operate within what we would consider to be the normal range of a democracy?

The idea of stress driving a system beyond some normal range of operation is at least applicable to given types of systems. It is certainly implicit in much of the analysis traditionally undertaken with respect to them. Theoretically, the identification of a point of stress is relatively simple for given types. Any time a disturbance leads to the change of the essential characteristics of a type of system—those that best define the characteristic way in which the system operates—we can say that the system has been put under stress and has succumbed to it. Empirically it might be somewhat more difficult to establish when this point has been reached. Even here the contrasts are clear; it is only the thresholds that would remain ambiguous. Certainly, if Spain were to introduce free popular elections and freedom of speech and association in the Western pattern or if the French regime were to restore the Presidency to a less dominant role and parties to a more prominent one, there would be little question that the systems fell within what would be explicitly considered the normal range of variation of a democratic system.

Essential variables as indicators of stress

If, temporarily, we continue to use given types of systems as a point of departure, it is clear that latent in our description of them as operating within a normal range, beyond which stress may push them, is the idea that there are certain *essential variables*[8] that are thus being displaced beyond

---

[8] This concept has been adapted from W. R. Ashby, *An Introduction to Cybernetics* (New York: John Wiley & Sons, Inc., 1956), p. 197.

their normal range. For democracies these might be conceived to be some vaguely defined degree of freedom of speech and association and popular participation in the political process. For a totalitarian system the essential variables might consist of some minimal degree of exclusion of popular participation, dominant power in the hands of a political elite, coercion of the individual, and controlled and highly restricted freedom of speech and association. But our criteria for classifying political systems are sufficiently imprecise to leave considerable room for dispute as to what the essential variables are that help to distinguish one type of system from another.

Regardless of the theoretical problems of classification encountered in any effort to single out the essential identifying variables of a particular type of system, we tend to operate on the assumption that it is possible to distinguish two different aspects of a system. The one identifies those features of a system that enable it to operate in a characteristic way and that thereby distinguish it fundamentally from other systems. By classifying systems as democratic, authoritarian, totalitarian, traditional, or modernizing, we are attributing to each type of system different characteristic modes of operation. Presumably, this difference can be specified through the kinds of relationships or patterns of interaction that we consider central properties of the system. We may call these differences, whatever their specific character may be, the essential variables.

In most types of systems the system will retain its characteristic properties, say, as a democracy or totalitarian system, as long as the essential variables remain within a given range, what I have called the normal range. Again, empirically it may be difficult to discern when the system is moving toward the critical point, one beyond which it becomes transformed into a different system. For some observers Gaullist France has moved beyond the critical limits of a democracy; but persons may differ at least empirically on this score. However, theoretically it is clear that the essential variables of a type of system need not just be present or absent. They will usually be of a type that can be present in greater or lesser degree. Only when they function within some normal or critical range can the system be described as conforming to the criteria of a given type. For example, if a system is to be labeled democratic, the presence in politics of freedom of speech or popular participation in a small measure may not be enough. The amount is critical. Few systems eliminate all freedom, and in modern mass societies, some forms of popular participation are almost mandatory.

The persistence of a given type of political system requires more than the presence of essential variables. They need to operate above a certain level. In other words, there is a critical range and if disturbances displace the system beyond it, the entire system will change its character.

By implication, there must be a second aspect to systems. This aspect may change without altering the characteristic mode of operation of the system. It will consist of the nonessential features of a system. For example, in light of the customary classification I am using, the United States would continue to function characteristically as a democracy regardless of the many changes in its political structure in the last fifty years. Many modifications in a type of political system are possible without leading to the transformation of the type.

Perhaps an illustration from biology will help to illuminate the difference between essential and nonessential variables. Let us turn to the human organism, if we may do so without being accused of thinking that a political system corresponds in most respects to this biological system. Changes in certain variables internal to the organic system may occur without destroying the normal mode of operation of the body as a whole. The loss of an eye, a limb, or other duplicated organs may reduce the flexibility with which the organism can cope with any succeeding disturbances, but it need not destroy the typical way in which the organism functions. We may describe this situation by saying that the essential variables of the organic system have remained within their normal range. If the blood pressure had been displaced beyond a certain level or the sugar content of the blood fell below a specified point, there would be more serious consequences. These constitute two essential variables of the organic system that must be kept within critical limits if the system as a whole is to persist.

Stress and the critical limits
of the essential variables

Once we recognize that there is this difference between variables essential to the characteristic mode of operation of a system and those that are of secondary importance and that the former operate within normal ranges, we have a clue toward a useful way of describing stress on a system. It can now be said to be a condition that occurs when disturbances, internal or external in origin, threaten to displace the essential variables of a political system beyond their normal range and toward some critical limit. Thereby it prevents a political system from operating in its characteristic way.

Two things need to be said about this description of the stress potential of a disturbance. First, empirically we may not have adequate measures or indices of when a disturbance becomes stressful and threatens to destroy a system. But, as I have indicated, the task of theory is to point out what is necessary. As long as in principle it is possible to achieve, empirically, what is necessary, it becomes a separate although important matter to locate empirical indicators of theoretically important phenomena. No more than at many other points in our analysis need we be perturbed here by the current lack of such indicators.

Second, since stress is a potential in the form of a present danger or threat, we may need to assess a disturbance as stressful even though the essential variables do not pass beyond their critical limits. The fact that such a stressful disturbance did not push the essential variables this far would not necessarily be proof of an erroneous assessment. It could be an indication that at some point the members of a system were able to intervene constructively so as to prevent the disturbance from continuing to operate in a stressful manner, at least to the point of destroying the system. This is typically what happens when political systems do survive; every persisting system has homeostatic devices to help it cope with stress. But as long as a disturbance hinders rather than helps an essential variable, we may consider it to be stressful.

To reiterate, not every disturbance need result in stressing a system. Some may, in fact, reinforce the operation of its essential variables within the normal range and thereby help the system to continue functioning in its typical way. Let us return to democracy as a type of system for purposes of this illustration. If we accept the plausible hypothesis that the conditions for the functioning of democracy include a high level of literacy, acceptance of negotiation and compromise in the general culture, minimal levels of economic productivity, and the emergence of a strong middle class, changes among the parametric systems that encourage these conditions may well increase the probability that the essential variables of an existing democratic system will continue to operate within their normal range. By virtue of the same argument, any movement of these parameters in opposite directions will act as disturbances on a democratic system and will impose stressful consequences.

The essential variables of
political systems as such

Whatever the situation may be with regard to the ease of identifying stress in particular types of systems, it is now time to recall that our primary focus is not on the persistence of such types. Rather, it concerns any and all systems, regardless of type. How shall we establish when the capacity of a political system to continue as such a system is being put under stress, regardless of the capacity of the society to sustain any particular kind of political system? That is to say, if a political system under stress transforms itself from a democratic to a totalitarian one or from a weak to a strong presidential democratic system, the capacity of the society to sustain some kind of political system has not been impaired. However, if one after another kind of political system were tried and found wanting, it is conceivable that the members of the society might find themselves unable to support any political system, regardless of type. This would result in the destruction of all political life for that society and without doubt, the demise of the society as well. The very life processes of any political system in that society would be extinguished.

What, then, are the essential variables, not of a given type of system, but of any and all systems? When posed in this way, the question virtually answers itself. I have already identified a political system as those patterns of interaction through which values are allocated for a society and these allocations are accepted as authoritative by most persons in the society most of the time. It is through the presence of activities that fulfill these two basic functions that a society can commit the resources and energies of its members in the settlement of differences that cannot be autonomously resolved.

By definition, therefore, whatever type of system we may be considering, its characteristic mode of behaving as a political system, as contrasted, say, with an economic or religious system, will depend upon the capacity of the system to allocate values for the society and assure their acceptance. It is these two major variables or sets of variables—the behavior related to the capacity to make decisions for the society and the probability of their frequent acceptance by most members as authoritative—that are the essential variables and that therefore distinguish political systems from all other types of social systems. Once events occur leaving it impossible for members of a system to arrive at political decisions, or, if after they have been taken, they are regularly rejected by large segments of the membership, no political system (democratic, totalitarian, or authoritarian) can function. The system must either crumble into a variety of smaller units as seemed to be threatening in the Congo during the sixties, or it must be absorbed into another society subject to a different political system.

From this point of view all other variables may be considered non-essential or incidental. It must be emphasized that if we were directing our attention to an analysis of varying classes of systems, such as democracies, we would redefine the essential variables to include whatever characteristic patterns of political relationships we associated with this kind of system. But if we continue to take as our level of analysis the persistence of some kind of political system, regardless of the type involved—that is, the study of the underlying processes of all political life—the variables essential to the persistence of a specific type, such as democracy, become incidental with respect to all types of political systems considered as a species of social system. Thus, we establish the two essential variables for all and any kinds of political system as "the making and execution of decisions for a society" and "their relative frequency of acceptance as authoritative or binding by the bulk of society."

The normal range of the critical variables

The operation of essential variables need not be an all or nothing matter. A system may be more or less able to make decisions, put them into effect, and get them accepted as binding. The behavior involved varies on a range of effectiveness, and within that normal range a system may be able to persist. Thus, the authorities are not always able to make decisions; varying degrees of paralysis may occur as the history of the Weimar Republic and of France during the Third and Fourth Republics so clearly indicates. It is always a question of whether the capacity to make decisions has dropped below some critical point. Such a condition would signalize the loss of power to make some presently indeterminable minimum of decisions for the given system. Beyond that point the system disappears since it is no longer minimally effective in resolving differences among the members of a system. The critical point will vary with type of system and with time and place; in general, we would need to bear in mind that each system or type of system does have a critical point.

Similarly, even where the authorities are fully capable of making decisions and of seeking to implement them, compliance will vary on a continuum. The probability of the members accepting all decisions as binding is usually less than one, at least in any significant historical interval of time. Yet it must certainly be higher than .5. A system would be in a state of constant turmoil and confusion and might well be on the threshold of disappearance if there were just an equal probability that the decisions and associated actions of its authorities would be accepted or rejected. The ratio of rejection to acceptance must fall within a limited range well above that of chance. Below that level the system would collapse for want of sufficient authority being attached to its allocations.

Accordingly, as long as the disturbances operating on a system lead to changes in the system that do not affect its capacity to maintain these two essential variables within their indeterminate but, in principle, determinable normal range, they will not be considered stressful. They will, rather, just induce changes in the state of the system. The system may change, but not in any way that affects its characteristic mode of functioning as a political system. Where the disturbance can be interpreted as introducing changes in a system that are driving either of the essential variables beyond their critical range, we can designate them as stressful. If the disturbances can just be assessed as having the potential for doing so, that is, as representing a threat or pressure in that direction, they will also be noted as stressful.

It will be crucial to bear in mind the distinction I am attempting to make between the persistence of a type of system such as a democracy and any or all systems. It is easy to slip from the general to the type level, that is, from all and any systems to a special type such as democracy. Indeed, it is hard to resist the temptation to drop to a lower level of generality because, typically, in thinking about political life, political science has been concerned with the conditions for survival of democratic systems of varying subtypes and with the conditions for the elimination or self-destruction of dictatorial or nondemocratic systems of equally varying subtypes. From a policy-oriented point of view, and in the light of many alternative kinds of ethical considerations, this is as it should be. However, from the perspective of seeking to develop general theory, we are setting aside such ethically oriented questions. It should be evident that this is not because they are unimportant questions, but because in terms of the strategy of research the ethical and policy considerations will ultimately be better and more reliably answered if we have useful general theory as a point of departure.[9]

In any event, in view of my focus on general theory, it will be vital to bear in mind that what I designate as stressful for political systems as such will necessarily be equally so for any type. The converse, though, is not equally true. Disturbances stressful to a particular type of system need not be stressful to the essential variables of the political system as such. The destruction of the system type may well be one way of coping with stress so that at least *some* kind of system will endure. This need not mean that alternative methods for coping with the stressful disturbances are lacking. No one can say that the Nazi regime presented the only alternative to the Weimar Republic as a means of sustaining the essential variables of a German political system. There were probably many alternative ways of keeping the essential variables within their critical range. Even if there were not, the fact that systems analysis leads to a discussion of how systems typically seek to avoid stress is no indication that any outcome, even if it is the only one possible, is necessarily desirable according to my own value criteria. Both the ethical value of the transformations in a system and their impact on the probabilities of survival are vital considerations; at the same time they can be treated as quite different and separate matters.

THE REGULATION OF STRESS

Persistence in a stable or changing world will thus be found to be in part a function of the presence of stressful disturbances. We have seen that it is in the very nature of political life that these cannot be avoided. But the consequences of disturbances on the fortunes of the system itself—whether

[9] See my volume, *The Political System,* where this point is fully developed.

it survives and in what form—will depend upon the capacity and readiness of a system to cope with such stress.

It is a critical property of social systems, including political systems, that they are able to respond to the influences acting upon them. They can cope with such disturbances and seek to regulate them in some way. The members of a political system need not sit back, as it were, to accept stress supinely, through some mechanistically conceived way of adapting to changes taking place in the environment. This is what has long been unwittingly implied in equilibrium analysis as a theory of political life, a kind of conceptual posture that has been characteristic of much political research in the last half century.[10] The members of a system are able to react constructively in one or all of several directions so as to regulate the disturbances that have been thrust upon the system and, thereby, to seek to alleviate existing or potential stress.

Over time political systems in general, and each system in particular, have developed extensive repertoires of techniques for coping with possible stress. It is the fact that social systems have such repertoires at their disposal that dramatically distinguishes them from other kinds of systems. It builds a flexibility into them that not even the most complex biological systems, and therefore the most versatile of them, have ever possessed.

Although I shall reserve for a succeeding volume my discussion of the particular kinds of regulative responses that characterize all systems, here it will be useful to point to the general classes of responses that are to be found. Like human biological systems, political systems may be able to keep themselves intact, at least for brief periods, by insulating themselves from all change. Like human biological systems, political systems may even seek to control environmental and internal changes in such a way that they do not become stressful; or if they have already become so, so as to ward off the dangers already present.

What political systems as a type of social system possess uniquely, when compared to both biological and mechanical systems, is the capacity to transform themselves, their goals, practices, and the very structure of their internal organization. To keep the vital processes, the essential variables, of a political system alive, as it were, a system may remodel its structures and processes to the point where they are unrecognizable. A democracy may become transformed into an unmitigated dictatorship, a traditional system into a wholly modern one. No human biological system has yet been able to emulate this kind of self-transforming feat; although with modern computer technology and with a growing knowledge of the genetic structure, controlled

[10] I have dealt with "equilibrium" as a central theoretical concept in *The Political System, ad hoc* and in "Limits of the Equilibrium Model in Social Research," *Behavioral Science*, 1 (1956), 96-104.

mutation is well within the realm of probability. It may open up a modest range of internal reorganization of the human anatomy and physiological processes that will bring the biological system closer to the self-regulative potentials of a social system.

What is implied in these remarks is the presence of a capacity to call up a variety of responses in defense of the essential variable. What has been obscured is that the selection of alternatives from the repertoires is not necessarily given. The members may be able to make choices and vary their strategies within the limits permitted by circumstances. In one system an outbreak of violence may be the response to stress from deep and intransigent economic crises; in another system similar or even more severe economic disorganization may lead only to expressions of discontent in acceptable styles, accompanied by an intensification of corrective policies.

Not only is there freedom to select from a range of alternative strategies, but in many systems, at least those not bound by traditional practices, the members may consciously set out to devise new methods for meeting new or old crises. In this event they will be adding to their store of responses through innovation. In the last analysis as many alternative responses would be available to meet a stressful situation as can be suggested by the ingenuity of man. In this sense, once again, unlike the implications of the equilibrium model of political processes, the members of a system need not simply absorb a disturbance and mechanically seek to re-establish some old point of stability in the political system or move on to a new one. To accept a conceptualization of this sort would indeed be to leave the system in the hands of some invisible political hand. Members of a system have options, and within the range of these options alternative consequences for the persistence of the system may ensue. As one of these choices, and a central one for social systems, the members may search out entirely new avenues for meeting even old kinds of stresses. Adaptation, if one wished to attach this label to this process, becomes a creative and constructive task, informed with goals and direction.

It lies beyond the objectives of this volume to dip even lightly into the actual ways in which systems have sought to cope with stress or, for that matter, even into the major types of stress to which political systems from time immemorial have been exposed. The construction of a conceptual apparatus for these purposes will form the central theme of a succeeding volume.

Even if we shall not be delving into these problems, it is evident that before we could ever proceed to discuss the way systems typically handle stress, we would need to have at hand concepts satisfactory for detecting and analyzing the way in which disturbances impose themselves upon a system.

Although current research would seem unwittingly to imply otherwise, we cannot at all take it for granted that it is a simple or common-sense matter to trace out the way in which disturbances communicate themselves to political systems. When we inquire into this in the next chapter, we shall find that we have to generate special concepts to help us in this task. I shall identify these as inputs and outputs, and it is to their discussion that I turn.

SEVEN

The Political System Under Stress

How are we to detect the way in which disturbances affect the functioning of a system? Political research has tended to ignore this matter or to assume that there is no special problem in linking up events in the environment with the structures and processes within a political system. What may normally be taken for granted, we shall find rewarding to consider problematic. Indeed, we shall discover that the very method that we find useful for tracing the impact of disturbances upon a political system will also provide us with vital and theoretically manageable indicators of stress. In this chapter I shall examine concepts that will help us to reveal and analyze the precise way in which events and conditions in the environment are transmitted to the political system as potential sources of stress.

THE COMMUNICATION OF DISTURBANCES
TO THE POLITICAL SYSTEM

Environmental disturbances due to change

I shall begin in a relatively simple way. We are trying to understand how any political system manages to persist. We assume that it is subject to influences of many kinds coming to it from the environment or from things that happen within a political system. These have already been designated as disturbances. It is one thing to recognize generally that a system may be subject to such influences; it is quite another to devise categories of analysis that will enable us to handle the complexities involved in their transmission to the political system.

Because of the magnitude of the task, for the moment I shall neglect the disturbances occurring within a system and consider only those arising in the environment, especially the intrasocietal part. It is legitimate to do this because theoretically the problems of handling internal and external disturbances have a similar status and will therefore require no special analytic tools.

I shall set out by assuming, for illustrative purposes, that the environmental systems are themselves undergoing considerable change. How are we to link these changes to their consequences for a political system?

For example, it has become commonplace to emphasize the major problems confronting the erstwhile traditional societies resulting from their slow exposure to industrialized civilizations over earlier centuries and the suddenly increased rate and intensity of contacts today. It has led through a complex interlocking of influences to the emergence of new national units in unprecedented numbers; the relocation of populations in overcrowded, tense urban centers; the growth of an elite educated in the ideals of Western civilization; the slow downward percolation of these ideas to the broad indigenous populations; and the implanting of new scales of values associated with the disappearance of a subsistence economy and the spread of cash crops. A money economy, mobility of persons, and new ideals and goals for the individual and for the collectivities have all encouraged the importation and adoption of new technical skills. These have been found critical both to man the developing industrial complex, which may be slow in coming, and to mobilize the members of society in the pursuit of newly discovered ambitions and possibilities. Change has meant a not-so-slow awakening to the potency of organized behavior through trade unions, political parties, and tribal- or ethnic-based groups. It is compelling as well the adoption of rationally oriented bureaucratic structures for the achievement of both economic and political goals.

All of the societal changes mentioned have been or can be shown to have decisive effects on the way in which a political system operates. In many cases, with respect to the developing nations, especially in Africa, they have led to such stress on indigenous political systems that these systems have been unable to cope with the disturbances. The old tribal systems, already somewhat atrophied through varying colonial policies, are simply disappearing, if slowly. There can be little doubt that they will be fully absorbed, in most cases, into secular systems territorially based and bureaucratically organized.

If we sought to link these changes in the environment of a system—in its economy, culture, and social structure—to the destiny of the political system involved, we could continue to list the various elements in the environment that were undergoing change. We could link them on an *ad hoc* basis to the results they seemed to have for the structures and processes of the relevant political systems. Depending upon our interests, we could write volumes to show how change and development, whether in new or old nations, have led to the emergence of parties, legislatures, new patterns of political recruitment, new kinds of political motivations, special forms of interest groups, different kinds of political participation and involvement from what we are familiar with in the West, and novel methods of political leadership and control. But, in the end, we would still be faced with the need to bring some over-all order out of the welter of descriptive material and partial theories or so-called theories of interest groups, parties, personalities, or structural political change in developing areas that might have been evolved. At least, we would require an order that derives from more than the fact that the investigations deal with what all observers would agree are important transformations of political life attributable to changing environmental conditions.

We might seek to bring some theoretical order to the data by postulating functional requirements, substitutability of structures, and the comparison of varying structures for the fulfillment of constant functions. However scientifically valid such an approach may be, it has finally and conclusively been demonstrated to be at best theoretically trivial.[1] At worst, it involves the research worker in a gigantic numbers game to which there is no end: each investigator is encouraged to establish his own favored number of invariant functions and there is no satisfactory way of selecting among the alternatives.[2]

To the extent that there is any validity to the approach, it derives from the fact that it clarifies what lies at the base of all scientific research. Any inquiry postulates some kinds of functions, even though the exact term may not and need not be used. For this reason, the explicit identification of function does not indicate the presence of any special theory. It reflects only a scientific posture, which, of course, is to be encouraged. It also indicates a specific point of departure for theory construction. To stop there and simply compare alternative structures is to leave us waiting in suspense for the "dropping of the next shoe," namely, some kind of theory.

[1] K. Davis, "The Myth of Functional Analysis."
[2] I too have tried my hand at this "numbers game," as in my article "Political Anthropology" previously cited.

Even to begin to develop theoretical inquiry, it is necessary to go far beyond the relating of varying structures to functions. The order that functional analysis, at least as it has been vaguely outlined in political science, seeks to bring to comparative research, still leaves the basic problems of theory construction entirely untouched and could even do harm if unwittingly it were allowed to stand as an easy substitute for theorizing. It does not offer, at the minimum, a way of ordering data based upon a coherent and consistent body of concepts other than so-called functional terms that are and must be common to all scientific inquiry. Aside from these more general considerations, the so-called functional approach would still leave us struggling for a way of systematically working out the relationships between environmental changes and responses within political systems.

Stability as a special case of change

Even if we drop the assumption that change is taking place in the environment and turn to systems whose environments have been relatively stable (an exception in the modern world but frequent in the past and undoubtedly possible episodically in the future), we continue to face the problem of how to deal economically and systematically with influences on a system that come from the environment. Whether a system is imbedded in a constantly changing environment or in a stable one, the elements of the environment continue to exert an effect upon the operations of the system. The analysis of the effect of the stable environment on a system poses the same theoretical problems as in the case of rapidly changing ones, even though the rate of change may have important additional consequences.

Although social science has recently and suddenly become enamored of problems of change and a tidal wave of theories of change threatens to engulf us, it has at least opened our eyes to the fact that any general theory, if it is even minimally adequate, must be able to handle change as easily as it does stability.[3] But the truth is that in the elaboration of the initial fundamental categories of an analysis, there is no need for special concepts to study change. Indeed to introduce them would be a sign of weakness and a disjunction in the theory, not one of strength and integration.

Stability is only a special example of change, not a generically different one. There is never a social situation in which the patterns of interaction are absolutely unchanging. If stability is to have any sensible meaning, it must represent a condition in which the rate of change is slow enough to create

---

[3] I am here using the concept "change" in the usual loose sense of social science. The fact is that stability is not related to change or its antithesis. For the difference between static as against changing conditions on the one hand and stability on the other, see my previously cited article "Limits of the Equilibrium Model in Social Research."

no special problems due to change. But some change there always is. Hence, the study of stable systems involves a special case of change, one where the rate is slow. Similarly, so-called change draws attention to another special case in which the rate is high enough to create special consequences of which it is necessary to take note, both analytically and empirically.

Any general theory or conceptual framework, however, should be able to take both special cases simultaneously in its stride. The vital objective at the outset is not to create a special set of categories to examine special cases but, rather, to develop a set that will be useful for identifying the major variables involved in the functioning of the system, regardless for the moment of the rate of change. Whether a system is changing imperceptibly and is, therefore, said to be stable or whether it is changing rapidly and is, therefore, characterized as unstable or in transition does not alter the nature of the fundamental variables that need to be examined. It may add to them, but it cannot detract from them. The categories presented below are designed to be of this generic character.

Environmental disturbances under conditions of stability

Even under conditions of stability, where the rate of change is low, interaction between the environment and a system continues to occur. Hence, even if a special theory of change were required, it could not eliminate the similarity between change and nonchange with respect to the continuing presence of exchanges between a political system and its environment.

To illustrate, let us assume that we were interested in tracing out the consequences of social stratification upon the political structure. At one point, where a change had taken place in the social structure, we might discover that the realignment of social classes had modified the distribution of power in society in such a way that a new political elite had displaced the old one. The French and Russian Revolutions both led to consequences such as these. But once these effects on the political system had been produced, this did not lead to the elimination of the effects of the new class structure on the society, even if the new class relationship remained absolutely static. Once a change is introduced and stabilized, it may continue to exert its influence on other aspects of society. It is not like a bolt of lightning that does its damage and disappears to leave a single deposit of effects. Rather, it constitutes a continuing pressure on the political system.

The new status and class structure of the society would exert its continuing pressure on the political structure in many ways. It might affect the kind of persons recruited to political positions, the variety of issues raised for discussion, and the kind of decisions actually adopted and implemented. The absence of change implies not that politics escapes the influence of its parameters, but the stabilization of these influences. In other words, the exchanges between an environment and the political system imbedded in it continue, but without important modification.

It is vital to realize this fact. Even under the unreal state of absolutely static conditions in the environment of a political system, transactions between the two would still take place. If it were otherwise, we could never understand how a system could experience stress even if its conditions of existence did not change. If the conditions themselves have always been stressful, a system could be destroyed, not as a result of new kinds of stress occurring, but as a consequence of the failure of the members of the system at some point to handle the old and stable kinds as adequately as their predecessors.

THE LINKAGE VARIABLES BETWEEN SYSTEM AND ENVIRONMENT

Two things are clear from the preceding discussion. First, there is an enormous variety of influences coming from the environment of a political system capable of disturbing the way in which the system performs its tasks. Second, these influences are there whether the environment is relatively stable or fluctuating wildly. Environmental change which draws so much attention today, and appropriately so, does not create entirely new theoretical problems in the construction of a general structure of analysis. It simply aggravates an analytic problem that is already present, namely: How are we to systematize our understanding of the way in which the disturbances or influences from the environment are transferred to a political system? Do we have to treat each change or disturbance as a particular or general type, as the case may be, and simply work out its specific effects in each instance? If so, because of the obviously enormous variety of influences at work, the problems for systematic analysis are virtually insurmountable. But if we can discover a way of generalizing our method for handling the impact of the environment on a system, there would be some hope for reducing the enormous variety of influences into a relatively few and, therefore, relatively manageable number of indicators or variables. This is precisely what I shall seek to do.

Transactions across system boundaries

Since we have been conceiving of a political system as analytically separable from all other social systems, and frequently empirically differentiated as well through an independent political structure, it is useful to treat the disturbances or influences occurring from behavior in the environmental systems as *exchanges or transactions* that cross the boundaries of the political system. None of the broad social systems into which I have classified the environment stands completely independent of the other; complex interpenetration occurs. That is, each is coupled to the other in some way, however slight it may be. Exchanges can be used when we wish to refer to the mutuality of the relationship, that is, where each has a reciprocal influence on the other. Transaction may be used when we wish to emphasize the movement of an effect in one direction, simply across the boundary from one system to another.[4]

However scientifically important it may be to point this out, by itself the statement is so obvious as to have little interest. What can and will carry recognition of this coupling beyond a mere truism is the invention of a way to trace out the complex exchanges so that we can readily reduce the immense variety of interactions to theoretically and empirically manageable proportions.

In order to accomplish this, I propose to reduce the major and significant environmental influences to a few indicators. Through the examination of these we should be able to appraise and follow through the potential impact of environmental events on the system. With this objective in mind, I shall designate the effects that are transmitted across the boundary of a system toward some other system as the *outputs* of the first system and, hence, as the *inputs* of the second system, the one that they influence. A transaction between systems will therefore be viewed as a linkage between them in the form of an input-output relationship.

If we now apply this general conceptualization of the points of linkage between systems to a political system and its environmental systems, it offers us a rudimentary model of the type illustrated in Diagram 2. This is, of course, a gargantuan oversimplification both of reality and of my developing conceptual scheme itself. But the task of analysis is at least to begin by stripping away all incidental relationships in order to lay bare the essential framework. These are the very minimal commitments if we inquire into political life as a system of behavior. In a succeeding volume the objective

---

4 Exchange is sometimes used to suggest some kind of mutually beneficial relationship such as a settlement or contractual tie in which each of the parties feels there is something to be gained. I presume that Talcott Parsons typically uses the concept in this or in a closely related sense. See his use of the term in *The Social System* (New York: Free Press of Glencoe, Inc., 1951), especially at pp. 122 ff and in a volume with N. J. Smelser, *Economy and Society* (New York: Free Press of Glencoe, Inc., 1956), pp. 105 and 184. Here, however, I shall confine the term to a neutral meaning, one that denotes only that events in two or more systems have reciprocal effects on the systems involved and that these effects are not unrelated to each other. Interaction might well have been used to describe the relationship except that it has been customary to restrict this concept to the actions and reactions among social roles rather than among systems.

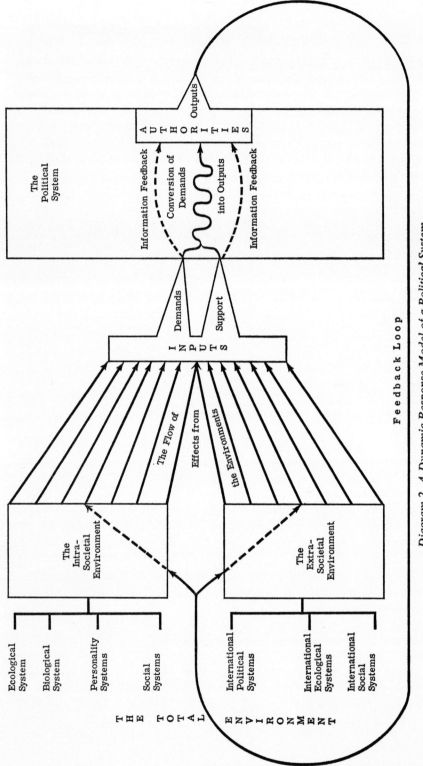

The Political System

Information Feedback

Conversion of Demands into Outputs

Information Feedback

A U T H O R I T I E S

Outputs

Demands

Support

I N P U T S

The Flow of

Effects from

the Environments

The Intra-Societal Environment

The Extra-Societal Environment

Ecological System

Biological System

Personality Systems

Social Systems

International Political Systems

International Ecological Systems

International Social Systems

T H E   T O T A L   E N V I R O N M E N T

Feedback Loop

Diagram 2. A Dynamic Response Model of a Political System.

will be to add complicating relationships of various sorts so that the model will offer a somewhat closer approximation to the relationships in phenomenal systems. Here the analysis will remain macroscopic in intent. We shall be observing political systems from a considerable distance, as through a telescope rather than a microscope. This is in the nature of the case, given the present state of theoretical analysis in political research. Although we have much empirical detail, we have tended to lose sight of the need to see the outlines of the over-all picture.

A flow model of the political system

Broadly, this diagramatic representation of the functioning of a political system suggests that what is happening in the environment affects the political system through the kinds of influences that flow into the system. Through its structures and processes the system then acts on these intakes in such a way that they are converted into outputs. These are the authoritative decisions and their implementation. The outputs return to the systems in the environment, or, in many cases, they may turn directly and without intermediaries back upon the system itself. In Diagram 2 on page 110 the arrows from the environments portray the vast variety of transactions between them and the political system. Here, though, the arrows have only single heads, and they are shown in such a way that they are fed into the system in summary form as demands and support. The exchange or reciprocity of the relationship between the system and its environments, previously depicted as double-headed arrows, is now indicated by arrows that show the direction of flow of the outputs toward the environmental systems. This clearly demonstrates that the inputs of the environment are really just the outputs of the political system. The broken lines in the environmental systems reflect the dynamics of the relationship. They indicate that there is a continuous flow of influences or outputs from the political system into and through the environments. By modifying the environments, political outputs thereby influence the next round of effects that move from the environment back to the political system. In this way we can identify a continuous feedback loop. The meaning of the other lines and designations on the diagram will become apparent as our discussion proceeds.

As detailed as the diagram is, much is omitted, as we would expect. First, many other environmental systems could be added even to take into account the few that were identified in an earlier chapter. Second, the interrelationships among environmental systems themselves are completely omitted since they would have so cluttered the diagram as to leave it virtually indecipherable. Finally, the structures and processes through which a political system converts its inputs into outputs are represented only by the serpentine line within the system. It does suggest, however, that the various inputs from the external system are worked upon and converted into outputs that return to one or another of the external systems as inputs for them.

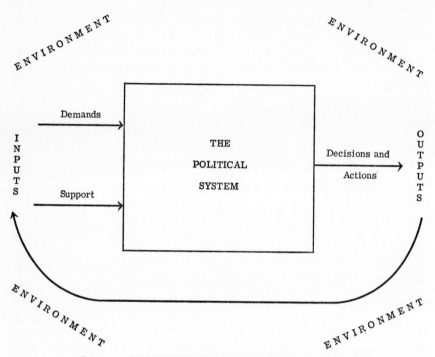

Diagram 3. A Simplified Model of a Political System.

Diagram 3 goes even further in stripping the rich and complex political processes down to their bare bones. It depicts in their simplest guise the dynamic relationships among the processes of a political system. It serves to dramatize an image to which we shall return; it reveals that, after all, in its elemental form a political system is just a means whereby certain kinds of inputs are converted into outputs. At least, this is a highly useful starting point from which to begin plugging in the complexities of political life.

THE INPUT VARIABLES

Demands and support as input indicators

The value of inputs as a concept is that through its use we shall find it possible to capture the effect of the enormous variety of events and conditions in the environment as they pertain to the persistence of a political system. Without the inputs it would be difficult to delineate in any precise operational way how behavior in the various sectors of society affects what happens in the political sector. Inputs will serve as summary variables that concentrate and reflect everything in the environment which is relevant to political stress. Because it is possible to use inputs in this manner, the concept can serve as a powerful analytic tool.

Whether or not we use inputs as summary variables will depend upon how we define them. We might conceive of them in their broadest sense. Then we would interpret them as including any event external to the system —confining ourselves momentarily to environmental inputs—that alters, modifies, or affects the system in any way. If inputs are used in such a broad sense, we could never exhaust the list of those that leave an impact on the political system. This is represented on Diagram 1, page 75. The double-headed arrows coupling environmental systems to the political system could be multiplied a thousandfold, and we would not have begun to skim the surface of the number and variety of influences flowing among these systems.

Let us take only a minute number of illustrations. The effect of the economy on creating and sustaining powerful economic classes, urbanization, interest group segmentation, fluctuations in the business cycle, and the like would constitute inputs, broadly interpreted, that shape the character of the political structure, the distribution of power therein, and the goals of political controversy. The general culture helps to mold the constraints within which political discussion and competition take place (if it is permitted at all), lends color to the style of political life, and signalizes the kinds of issues that will be considered important by the members of the system. Motivational patterns found in modal personality types or in elite personalities within a society will contribute to the availability of personnel to fill the political roles, to the incentives for political participation, and to the types that achieve leadership status and to their perception of policy. We could enlarge this list indefinitely. For each sector of the environment introduced we would need a separate partial theory to explain the effect which its inputs might have. The only unifying element in it all would be that we were seeking to trace out and interrelate the inputs (that is, the general and specific effects) of each of these parameters on a common object—the political system.

However, we can simplify enormously the task of analyzing the impact of the environment on the political systems if we adopt more narrowly defined inputs and use them as indicators that will sum up most of the important effects that cross the boundary between these systems. This conceptualization would relieve us of the need to deal with and trace out the effect on a system of every different type of environmental event separately.

As the analytic tool for this purpose, it is helpful to view the major parameters as focusing their effects on two major inputs: demands and support. Through them a vast range of changes in the environment may be channeled, reflected, and summarized. For this reason they can be used as the key indicators of the way in which environmental events and conditions modify and affect the operations of the political system. On Diagram 2, page 110, the multiple transactions are collapsed into two major inputs, and these alone are conceived as flowing into and affecting the political system.

It will matter little whether we consider these inputs as internal or external to the political system. They stand on the border, bridging and linking the political system with all other intra- and extrasocietal systems. Depending upon the requirements of our analysis, they may be equally conceived to lie within the system or outside it, as long as we recognize that they remain in the neighborhood of the boundary.

"Withinputs" as intrasystem indicators

At times I have been writing as though all the influences or disturbances that had to be considered in understanding how a system manages to persist occurred in the environment of a system. As we know from what has already been said, many of these influences may occur within a system itself. Insofar as things happening within a system shape its destinies as a system of inter-actions, it will be possible to take them into account as they are reflected through the inputs of the members of a system. It does not seem reasonable to speak of these events as inputs since they already occur within the system rather than outside. For the sake of logical consistency we might call them "withinputs." All that would be meant by this neologism is that we have decided to treat, in a unified way, the effects that events and conditions both within and without a system may have upon its persistence. Hence, unless the context requires otherwise, in writing of inputs I shall include "within-puts" in the same category.

We need to take the trouble to make the distinction because recognition of the two categories sensitizes us to the value of looking within the system as well as the environment to find the major influences that may lead to stress. Just as a human body may fail because of an infection received from the outside or from the attrition, through old age, of some organ such as the heart, a political system may suffer stress from disturbances in the environ-ment or from failures that can be attributed directly to processes or struc-tural arrangements within the system itself. For example, members of the American political system have from time to time felt that the whole regime has been threatened by the difficulties that the separation of powers has aggravated with regard to the passage of legislation. This is traditionally brought out in discussions of a responsible two-party system for the United States. To signalize the fact that the disturbance has occurred within the system and that the stressing input has been shaped by internal events, the concept "withinputs" can be used.

Illustrations of the summary
function of inputs

It will be helpful to have some brief indication of what demands and support comprise and how they could be used, although a full analysis of their role as summary variables through which stress is transmitted will have to await a later work. To take a specific example, let us assume that we are interested in a developing nation which is undergoing a transition from a tribal form of organization based upon village headmen, lineage elders, and a lineage-determined paramount chief with minimal power, toward a national political leadership based upon secular party organization, a legislature, an efficiency-oriented bureaucracy, and a dominant leadership. Presumably the modifications of the old tribal system have been brought about in part through contact with Western ideals of democracy and administration, buttressed by the needs of a changing economy and social structure.

In accordance with current procedures of political research, we might specify the aspect of political change that seems to be important. Normally we would use as the criteria of relevance those changes in the direction of or away from Western democratic institutions. We might then seek to account for the direction, rate, and outcome of these changes by considering all of the external changes that can then be shown to be relevant to the political changes which we have already selected as important according to these criteria.

From the perspectives of our analysis the environmental changes are considered to be disturbances on the existing tribal system because of the stress they impose upon it, leading ultimately to its transformation. In response to the stress the system either becomes extinct and is absorbed by some other society, or it responds and adapts by adopting modernized political structures in the shape of parties, legislatures, rationalized bureaucracy, and a generalized leadership (rather than a lineage, tribal, or ethnically based leadership).

The critical questions for us do not relate to the way in which environmental disturbances modify the particular form of the internal structures or processes of the system. Such changes may take place without any discernible effect upon the capacity of some kind of system to persist, or they may not be fundamentally related to this capacity. That is to say, whether the adopted modernized structure happens to be modeled after the British parliamentary system or the American presidential type may or may not have relevance to the capacity of some kind of system to persist. What is important is that the traditional political forms have given way to at least a semblance of the bureaucratized types. For us the critical questions are: To what extent did the disturbances constitute stress on the pre-existing system? Precisely how did this stress manifest and communicate itself? How did the system cope with this stress, if at all?

A useful way of answering such questions lies in exploring the impact that contacts with the West, both ideological and economical, have upon the inputs. Briefly, exposure to the kind of life possible under Western forms of social organization, together with the emergence of the material means through transition from a subsistence to a cash and wage economy, has unleashed a vast increase in the volume of demands which members of the system now seek to satisfy through political action. This in itself imposes such a severe burden on the old tribal forms of political organization that they could not possibly cope with them.

Further, the changes in the environment serve to broaden the types of demands for which satisfaction is now sought through the political system. Such new demands, at their most inclusive level, are typically capsulated into programs for national freedom and political unity among divergent groups, linked usually to policies advocating a rapid rate of economic development. The kinds of commitments required from the members of the system for the fulfillment of these types of demands are dramatically different from those required under the prior traditional systems. The novelty of the demands themselves create severe crises in the developing nations.

Changes in volume and variety of demands represent a major and fundamentally neglected type of stress that environmental changes may be interpreted as bringing to bear upon a political system. In this way a vast host of different kinds of changes such as these may be drawn together and observed through a single kind of variable, that is, as they influence the volume and variety of demands.

But something more is also at stake in these emerging national units. It is to be found in the need for a new leadership to weld together a group that can offer sufficient support for a new political unit, a new set of structures for getting things done politically, and new political authorities to provide leadership and administrative skills. These are the basic components of a political system which might be labeled the political community, regime, and authorities.[5] The search for rapid economic and social development,

---

[5] For a brief discussion of these terms see Easton, "An Approach to the Analysis of Political Systems," and "Political Anthropology." The concepts will be elaborated in detail in another volume.

combined with political stability, imposes on such systems the need to generate a leadership which can promote and sustain support for these components. To do so they may have to negotiate coalitions among the dominant ethnic, lineage, and new economic groups in the society. They may look for support among young adults, among the politically dispossessed tribes, or among the urban workers deprived of the past security of lineage ties. They may turn to the use of coercion.

However the new leadership may seek to renew the input of support for some system, stress owing to the decline of support for the pre-existing system can be laid at the door of environmental changes of the kinds already mentioned. Where the fact of change indicates that the old systems thereby failed, we can interpret the situation to mean that the members were able to assure the persistence of some kind of system by transforming themselves into and lending support to a modernizing or transitional type of system. Regardless of how the system coped with the stress, the point is that environmental disturbances can be summarized and unified through their influence on the level of support for a system. By thus utilizing support as the connecting link between the environment and a system, we obtain a clue about how this variable serves as the focal point of many different kinds of environmental changes important for an understanding of stress on a system.

A great deal more needs to be said about the way in which the inputs of demands and support sum up and reflect the changes taking place in the environment of a political system, communicate these changes as disturbances to the system, and in turn are acted upon by the system as a way of coping with potential stress. Final validation of the fact that most of the important aspects of environmental events and conditions are refracted through these two indicators will have to wait for the elaboration of each input and the system response. My purpose is to sketch out and offer only a preliminary view of the role that these inputs do play. Through the adoption of this kind of conceptualization we are able to invent a means for tracing out the way in which stress may be communicated to a system.

Few systems succumb to stress from a stable environment or even from a rapidly changing one. The fact that many systems are able to cope with the disturbances that may threaten the very existence of any system at all must lead us to inquire into the means whereby they have been able to do so. When we have done this in the next chapter, we shall have rounded out our introduction to the kinds of commitments which we may unwittingly be assuming once we begin to pursue consistently the theoretical implications already embodied in the idea of a system itself.

EIGHT

The Responding Political System

Thus far our attention has been concentrated on the way in which stress is communicated to a system. The discussion has demonstrated that if we wish to find out what happens to a political system, we must be prepared to take into account two separate kinds of events. An equation representing the factors at work would include not only indices of any threatening increase in volume of demands or decrease in support, but also the particular responses by a system. Where one system may be destroyed through failure to take the appropriate actions to alleviate the stress, another may sail smoothly on as a result of a reserve of past experience upon which it can draw for coping with the stressful conditions. Just as there is the need for concepts to order the experiences that lead to stress, in a systems approach there is a corresponding need for categories of analysis that will enable us to interpret the varying modes of response available to political systems.

TYPES OF REGULATIVE RESPONSES
TO DEMAND STRESS

Sources of demand stress

A system may be exposed to stress from demands in two ways. On the one hand, if the authorities in the system are unable or unwilling to meet the demands of the members in some determinable proportions (at least of those members who are politically potent), ultimately we could expect that this situation would breed a high and ever-increasing state of discontent. In due course, if demands continued to be thwarted or denied, the disaffection of the members who count might also spill over to the regime. Under certain circumstances parts of the membership might even seek to break away from the community in some kind of separatist movement.[1] *Output failure,* as we might call the result of this unwillingness or inability to meet demands, would tend in the direction of undermining support for the system, a characteristic kind of stress for a system. In this way we can see that, at least to the extent that demands are unfulfilled, they would have important consequences for the input of support.

On the other hand, demands may occasion stress on grounds quite independent of their impact on support. I alluded to this in the last chapter when I spoke of the stress due to an excessive volume and variety of demands. What is meant by this is that stress may occur because too many demands are being made; or their variety and content may be such that the conflict they stimulate requires an excessive amount of time to process. In either case it would be a matter of the system not having enough time to process the demands, assuming that demands cannot wait indefinitely before being met. We can, therefore, describe this condition of stress as demand-input overload.[2] Although this is not the place to explore the ramifications of this type of stress, a few remarks are in order if we are to appreciate the commitments involved in the kind of systems approach which we are exploring.

To begin with, stress due to input overload occurs as a result of the very simple fact that no system is able to accept and process through to outputs an unlimited number and variety of demands. By definition demands are articulated statements, directed toward the authorities, proposing that some kind of authoritative allocation ought to be undertaken. In some systems the members may be quite unaccustomed to imposing such demands, except perhaps in times of great crises. Many traditional systems with an unmobilized, apathetic, or impotent peasantry have been of this character.

---

[1] The American Civil War is a case in point. Continued dissatisfaction with outputs as they related to the demands from the South ultimately precipitated not only civil conflict but a demand for an entirely separate political system.

[2] J. G. Miller, "Information Input Overload and Psychopathology," *American Journal of Psychiatry,* 116 (1960), 695-704; "The Individual As An Information Processing System," in *Information Storage and Neural Control,* W. S. Fields and W. A. Abbott, eds. (Springfield, Ill.: Charles C. Thomas, Publisher, 1963), pp. 301-28; and "Information Input Overload," in *Self-Organizing Systems 1962,* M. C. Yovits, G. T. Jacobi, and G. D. Goldstein, eds. (Washington, D.C.: Spartan, 1962), pp. 61-78.

In other systems there may be little need for it, or the culture may prevail against many demands being made, as in those systems in the nineteenth century that were dominated for a short time by strong liberal or laissez-faire sentiments. But in many systems today and periodically in the past—as in the mercantilist period of Europe—a sufficient volume of demands is in fact directed toward the authorities so that a real problem is created as to whether the system can handle them. Indeed, one may well go further and ask the question as to whether all systems might not be confronted with an unmanageable flood of demands if it were not that various regulators are constantly at work to prevent this from happening.

Before looking at some of these, what could we expect would be the nature of the stress to which a system would be exposed if there were an unrestricted flow of demands to the authorities? The consequences are not difficult to imagine. As voiced indications of what the authorities ought to do, demands are messages. To reach their destination—in this case the authorities—messages must be able to flow along channels, whether they be by word of mouth, through mass media, correspondence, or the like. Regardless of the degree of structural differentiation and specialization in a system, no system is endowed with so many channels that it has an infinite capacity to carry demands. At some point, varying with the kind of system, its structure, and its culture, input overload of demands would occur.

A complete analysis of this phenomenon would require us to explore the conditions under which input overload could be expected to result. Suffice it to say here that we can visualize its possibility. To flavor the nature of a systems approach, what we need to question is whether systems can be shown to have devised typical ways for aborting such possible stress before it arises or alleviating its consequences if it seems imminent.

It is not likely that many systems have succumbed to the stress deriving from demand-input overload. Nevertheless, in many modern democracies it has often been argued that the heavy load that legislatures have to carry presents a real source of danger to the operations of that kind of system. Most modern systems are faced with the need to consider a staggering number of bills and decisions. By extension we could see that the same threat would confront any other type of political system that was compelled to try to process a greater volume of business than its organization permitted.

The argument about the potential dangers of demand overload does not rest upon evidence that it has in fact occurred. Even if it could be shown that no system has ever been so threatened, this does not of itself prove very much. It is still arguable that but for the universal precautionary measures systems do in fact take, such a threat would arise. The defenses that systems have built up against the input of excessive demands may be the very reason that few, if any of them, are completely destroyed through this kind of stress. If this is so, it makes an examination of these defenses more important than ever.

Regulation of demand stress

When we look at a political system from this perspective, we can immediately see that there are numerous devices the consequences of which could not be adequately understood unless we saw them as linked to the regulation of demand overload. In fact, they begin to operate at the very moment of the birth of a demand.

If we were to trace the career or progress of a demand in a system, we would find that at the outset, before it even becomes a demand, it appears in the form of a social want, preference, hope, expectation, or desire. With respect to these, we may at some moment come to think that action on the part of the authorities would be appropriate. It is only at that time—when our social wants or hopes are voiced as proposals for decision and action on the part of the authorities—that we need label them as political demands. It is at this very point of conversion into a political proposal for action that the first kind of important regulation of the volume and variety of demands may take place.

I can briefly illustrate what I mean by this if we look at some of the typical mechanisms. Thus, not all members are equally likely to give voice to a demand. Because of their general social status, some individuals or groups are more inclined to feel efficacious enough to articulate a political position. If this is so, persons occupying these roles in the social and political structure will have an important measure of control over the number of demands put into the system. For this reason we may call them structural regulators of the volume of demands; they are gatekeepers who stand athwart the admission channels to a system. In modern societies we may identify them as interest groups, parties, opinion leaders, or the mass media. In traditional societies they may take the form of notables, an aristocracy, or a military cadre. Whatever the particular form that these structural regulators take, it is clear that the volume or variety of demands that initially get into a system and begin to move along toward the point of output (the authorities) will depend upon the characteristics of these gatekeepers.

In addition to this limitation upon any indiscriminate input of demands, even at this stage in the progression of a demand, many cultural restraints will serve to modify the number of desires that members will even presume to convert to demands. In every system there are certain cultural inhibitions with regard to the kinds of wants for which a member feels it is appropriate to seek a political settlement. At one time it may be that aesthetic matters are not considered a subject for political action; at another, religion may be excluded as purely a subject of private concern; at still another, in a laissez-faire period, many kinds of economic wants may be left to members of the system to resolve without benefit of political intervention. Whatever the criteria of exclusion from political resolution may be, each system generates cultural restraints that help to keep the number of demands in leash at the very outset of their career, as they begin to take shape out of what are as yet nonpolitical wants, aspirations, or desires.

There are numerous other kinds of responses through which systems have typically sought to regulate potential demand overload. In all systems, it could be shown, processes are available through which the initial volume of demands that do manage to be voiced are themselves reduced in one way or another. We may describe this set of processes as the reduction of volume and variety through combination of two or more demands into one. Parties, interest groups, and opinion leaders in modern societies and comparable institutions in other systems perform this function. Part of their activities involves the synthesis and homogenization of demands so that from many of them it may be possible to develop a workable and simplified program of action and at the same time broaden the base of support for the group or individual. Regardless of the motivation behind efforts to weave together several demands into a common synthetic program, the consequence is that it leaves the system with fewer demands to handle.

However, more than this is required to reduce the volume of demands, particularly in modern systems. Typically, most systems under overload conditions have responded by increasing their channel capacity for bearing demands to the point where they become outputs. The channels for communicating demands play a vital function in helping a system cope with potential stress. For example, the very proliferation of political structures has meant that there are many more means through which demand can be processed. The fact that increasing structural differentiation has been accompanied by added specialization has also meant that these channels may remain open for what amounts to longer periods of time; they can thus handle a greater volume.

In this brief statement it is impossible to exhaust even a nominal description of the typical ways in which systems may respond to demand input overload. I have, however, dwelt on these responses long enough to exemplify what is meant by response to demand input overload. It thereby provides some inkling into the kind of concepts and orientations implicit in a systems approach as it moves into a more complicated phase of its analysis.

TYPES OF REGULATIVE RESPONSES
TO SUPPORT STRESS

We have noted that demands represent only one primary index that can be used to locate and identify the way in which environmental and internal disturbances may stress a system. Support for various aspects of a system, as for some kinds of authorities, the regime, or constitutional order, or for the political community itself represents the second major index of stress. Where such support threatens to fall below a minimal level, regardless of the cause, the system must either provide mechanisms to revive the flagging support or its days will be numbered. Responses to a decline in support have typically taken three important forms, and it is helpful to look at these to obtain an overview of the kinds of concepts that they suggest.

Structural regulation of support

A regulative response with regard to support may include efforts to change the structure and processes that characterize a particular type of political system. This is perhaps the most radical strategy. It requires the system to transform its goals and structures as a means of maintaining at least some kind of system for making authoritative allocations. I have already shown that among types of systems, social systems have the maximum degrees of freedom in rearranging their internal order to meet stress. When a system is in danger of such disorganization and chaos that the essential variables can no longer operate, if it adopts a new constitutional order (structure, norms, and goals) fundamentally different from the one that went before, we have an instance of self-transformation that helps to assure the persistence of a system for making authoritative allocations. We might designate this kind of response *structural regulation* of support.

Diffuse support

Less radical measures are available to all systems. Persistence in these cases does not demand the abandonment of the existing regime or its serious modification. A system may seek to instill in its members a high level of *diffuse support*[3] in order that regardless of what happens the members will

---

[3] Although support as a concept occurs frequently in political research, its use in this kind of context is designed to give it much more precision than is customarily the case and to provide it with broad theoretical significance. Its conscious use in a theoretical way has been suggested by Talcott Parsons in the previously cited article in Young, *Approaches to the Study of Politics*, although the categories proposed here and their specific meaning have been devised for my own special theoretical purposes.

continue to be bound to it by strong ties of loyalty and affection. This is a type of support that continues independently of the specific rewards which the member may feel he obtains from belonging to the system.

For generating this diffuse and generalized support the means may entail the positive encouragement of sentiments of legitimacy and compliance, the acceptance of a notion of the existence of a common good transcending the particular good of any particular individuals or groups, or the kindling of deep feelings of community. Thereby, sentiments of legitimacy, recognition of a general welfare, and a sense of political community are bred deeply into the maturing members of a system through the usual processes of political socialization and through the various special measures a system may adopt if it sees such support as declining.[4]

This reference to various types of responses through which a system might hope to sustain a high level of support for which the members require no particular *quid pro quo,* scarcely touches on the central function of these mechanisms as a means for aborting stress almost before it arises. It is enough for our present purposes, however, to accept the fact that no system could endure for very long if it did not seek to build up a reservoir of support—frequently described as patriotism, love of country, loyalty, and the like—upon which it could count regardless of the particular trials and tribulations or frustrations of desires that the members might experience at the moment.[5]

Outputs as a regulative mechanism

A final major category of response to support stress can be described as outputs. Through them, where diffuse support may threaten to fall to a dangerously low point, efforts may be made to stimulate the input of *specific support*. This is an input to a system that occurs as a return for the specific benefits and advantages that members of a system experience as part of their membership. It represents or reflects the satisfaction a member feels when he perceives his demands as having been met.

Not that any system can meet all the demands of its members; some must go unfulfilled. In some measure, where the demands put into the system

---

[4] I have dealt with some of the theoretical and empirical problems of political socialization in the following essays (with R. D. Hess): "The Child's Changing Image of the President," *Public Opinion Quarterly,* 24 (1960), 632-44; "Youth and the Political System" in *Culture and Social Character,* Lipset and Lowenthal, eds., pp. 226-51; "The Child's Political World," *Midwest Journal of Political Science,* 6 (1962), 229-46.

[5] Witness the efforts of every new political system to strengthen the ties to its members through "indoctrination," a form of socialization for support in which ideology plays a leading role.

are not met, discontent and even disaffection may be stimulated. Its consequences are always modified, however, by the overriding diffuse support that a member may have become accustomed to extend. Whatever the grievances a member expresses, he may still remain fundamentally true to the system.

But where a system consistently fails to meet those minimal demands that members have come to feel are their due—and what these are will vary with historical moment and culture—the system would find the input of specific support on the decline. It would have to rely increasingly on the general feelings of good will (diffuse support) entertained by the members. Consistent frustration of what are assessed as just wants, over longer periods of time, if not compensated for by an increase in the input of diffuse support, must lead to a degree of attrition in specific support that would fundamentally weaken the system. The lists of grievances, repeatedly presented to reigning European monarchs in earlier centuries, became known as harbingers of revolt or revolution.

Outputs may represent a central contribution, therefore, to the forces that help to sustain the essential variables of a system. A rounded analysis of a system would require an extended inquiry into their types and consequences. If through nothing else, the central relevance of outputs is revealed in the fact that in recent decades contemporary political science has shown a degree of interest in the way public policies are formed and executed that exceeds anything known in its past. And public policies may very loosely be conceived as one type of outputs from a system.

OUTPUTS

What are these outputs? This question allows us to look at exchanges between a system and its environment from a new perspective. We are able to see them as transactions moving from the system itself to its environment.

In every political system many kinds of events occur that have consequences for the environment. We might be tempted to identify all of these as the outputs. However, it will serve our analytic purposes better, as in the case of inputs, if we restrict outputs to a narrower meaning. The term will not be used to summate all events that take place in a system. It will be confined to those kinds of occurrences already described as authoritative allocations of values or binding decisions and the actions implementing and related to them.

In this sense outputs are exemplified in the statutes of a legal system, administrative decisions and actions, decrees, rules, and other enunciated policies on the part of the political authorities, the informal consensus of a clan council, and even favors and benefits from authorities. Just as inputs are a way of organizing and communicating the effects of environmental changes to the political system, outputs reverse the process. They represent a method for linking up what happens within a system to the environment through the unique behavior related to the authoritative allocation of values. They identify and summarize the effect that actions and events, of the kind specified, have on the environment and, at times, even directly upon the system itself, as the output arrows show on Diagram 2, page 110.

What are the processes through which outputs influence the level of specific support being put into a system? In and of themselves outputs have no consequences. They must alter existing conditions in some way or maintain them if but for the output they would have changed. At times, however, it may suffice for the outputs to be communicated to the members so that they may perceive that something is being done on their behalf.

Another way of stating this is to say that if outputs are to have any impact on support, in one or another way they must be able to meet the existing or anticipated demands of the members of a system. They will do this either by modifying environmental or intrasystem conditions so that the original circumstances that gave rise to the demands no longer exist, or they may take steps to create this impression in the minds of the members, even though in fact nothing other than the image has been changed. Failing this, the authorities through the outputs may coerce the members into continuing to support a system even though no efforts are made to satisfy their demands.

This statement about output effects raises many questions. To determine the consequences outputs have for support we would have to know whose demands need to be satisfied to maintain a level of support sufficient to enable a system to persist, how frequently this would have to occur, how many of the demands, even of these significant members, would have to be met, and the like. Regardless of these kinds of matters, the point that I wish to make here is simply that the capacity of a system to respond to stress (a property that distinguishes it as a system of behavior) can be exercised through its production of outputs. It would, therefore, be vital to trace out the consequences of these outputs as they affect the environment and the system itself and create the kinds of conditions that nurture or destroy supportive sentiments.

FEEDBACK

Even if they wished to, how are the authorities in a system to produce outputs that will regulate the volume of demands or maximize the input of support? How do they come to learn that some action is required on their part? How are they able to arrive at some judgment about what the right actions might be? In brief, if the members of a system, the authorities included, are to be able to respond to stress in such a way as to regulate it in any of the ways just described, what is there about a political system that allows them to make some efforts in this direction? This brings us to the core of the political system conceived as a self-regulating, self-directing set of behaviors.

In general terms, the capacity of a system to respond to stress will derive from two central processes found within it. Information about the state of the system and its environment can be communicated back to the authorities; through their actions the system is able to act so as to attempt to change or maintain any given condition in which the system may find itself. That is to say, a political system is endowed with feedback and the capacity to respond to it. It is through the combination of these properties—feedback and response—which until recent years had gone virtually unrecognized, that a system is able to make some effort to regulate stress by modifying or redirecting its own behavior.[6]

The content of feedback

If a system is to be able to respond and thereby seek to cope with stress, what kind of information must it be able to obtain? It is clear that, first, the authorities in the system, those invested with the special responsibilities and powers to act in the name of the system, would need to know the conditions prevailing in the environment as well as in the system itself. In this way they could act so as to anticipate any circumstances that might lead to the withdrawal of support, whether diffuse or specific. Not only will the authorities frequently have a better opportunity to maintain the input of support if actions are taken before stress-provoking conditions occur; at times it is mandatory that such anticipatory measures be taken.

Second, the authorities must also seek to acquire information about the supportive state of mind of the members and the demands being voiced at least by the politically influential members of the system. It is important to know whether the members are acquiescent to the regime and solidary with the political community or whether they are on the verge of revolt against both and what their specific demands are.

[6] An enormous literature has grown up in this area. A few works particularly relevant to the analysis of social systems may be mentioned here: Ashby, *An Introduction to Cybernetics* and *Design for a Brain* (New York: John Wiley & Sons, Inc., 1952); J. W. Forrester, *Industrial Dynamics* (New York: M.I.T. Press and John Wiley & Sons, Inc., 1961); Kuhn, *The Study of Society;* W. Sluckin, *Minds and Machines* (London: Penguin, 1954); G. Vickers, *The Undirected Society* (Toronto: University of Toronto Press, 1959); N. Wiener, *Cybernetics* (New York: John Wiley & Sons, Inc., and the Technology Press, 1948) and *The Human Use of Human Beings,* rev. ed. (New York: Doubleday & Company, Inc., an Anchor book, 1954).

Third, the authorities must obtain information about the effects which the outputs have already produced. But for this, the authorities would have to act in perpetual darkness. There must be a continuous flow of information back to them so that whatever their goals may be with respect to support or the fulfillment of demands, they are aware of the extent to which their prior or current outputs have succeeded in achieving these goals.

It is important to note that, with respect to the input of support, we cannot take the goals of the authorities for granted. The authorities need not always be eager to encourage support for a system, although typically they are likely to identify with the on-going system. However, in some instances the authorities may well be interested in modifying the system radically or destroying it entirely. It served Hitler's purposes to come to power under the guise of the Weimar Republic, but he was quick to reduce it to ashes and substitute the Third Reich. From his position of authority De Gaulle similarly succeeded in dislodging the residual support being tendered the Fourth Republic and in transforming it into a regime that reversed the relationship between the executive and the legislature. In cases such as these the information returning to the authorities would be used to undermine rather than strengthen the support for the old order.

Regardless of the specific goals of the authorities, however, the point is that if they are to be attained, there must be a flow of information, of the kinds described, coming back to them. Only on the basis of knowledge about what has taken place or about the current state of affairs with respect to demand and support would the authorities be able to respond by adjusting, modifying, or correcting previous decisions, including the failure to make a decision. Not that they must do so; but at least possession of the information provides them with the opportunity if they desire to use it. Without such feedback, behavior would be erratic or random, unrelated in any causal way to what had previously occurred.

The illustration of feedback processes appears on Diagram 2, page 110. The effects on outputs, shown in that diagram, flow back to the environment and move through the relevant systems there, as indicated by the broken lines in the environmental boxes on the diagram. The information about these consequences then returns from the environment to the system. Since the authorities are the producers of outputs, by definition, it is toward them that the feedback must flow if it is to be effective in enabling the system to meet stress from the decline of support. The whole network, from initial output point back to the authorities again, may be called the feedback loop.

Other aspects of feedback processes

In this volume I am concerned solely with the task of unveiling the commitments encountered in the adoption of a systems analysis; this obviates exploring the numerous complexities centering in the feedback processes. We would need to know, for example, what kind of information typically returns to the authorities along the feedback loop and the extent to which it is accurate, false, or distorted. To what degree do time leads and lags, the number of feedback channels, the length of these as transmission belts and their variety, influence the type of information fed back? To what extent is accuracy dependent upon the perceptual apparatus of the authorities and the way in which it may be influenced by ideology, prejudice, indifference, or lack of ability to obtain and interpret information? And even if the authorities do obtain accurate information, lack of will to use it, lack of resources to put it to use, inadequate wisdom and skills in doing so may all contribute as much to an inability to meet a decline in support as the absence of such information feedback itself. We would also need to inquire into the decision rules guiding the retrieval of information from the collective memory banks in which past experience is stored. The skill in utilizing past information as stored in memory will be intimately related to the wisdom of outputs with regard to current stress.

Whatever the complexities involved, it is apparent that feedback plays a prominent role in the way in which the members of a system meet stress. It also serves to sharpen our understanding of the special capacity that social systems as against all other types of systems have been shown to have. In order to preserve some system for making and implementing binding decisions, the authorities are able to respond to a low level of support by a variety of actions that are limited only by the inventive and combinational intellectual resources of men. Without feedback these potentials would be wasted; they could be used only randomly. Possessed of feedback information, the members of a system are able to infuse their efforts with direction and purpose. It is for reasons such as these that feedback has been recognized as a central phenomenon in human behavior, both individual and collective.[7]

STRESS AND THE CONVERSION PROCESS

The identification of inputs, outputs, and feedback and the indication of the functions that they play in relating a system to its environment, as well as to sources of stress generated within the system, permits us to redefine the interactions that constitute a political system. We may now con-

[7] We are fortunate in having many of the critical problems of feedback analysis with respect to social systems expounded by Karl W. Deutsch in many articles and most recently in *The Nerves of Government*. This volume appeared after the present manuscript was essentially complete and its existence now spares me the need to delve into the broader cybernetic background of this kind of approach.

ceive of the inputs of a system as the raw materials from which the outputs are manufactured. From among the variety of demands presented in a system, its members, particularly at times those who have the special responsibility of leadership, must select a few as the goals and objectives of the system and commit the limited resources of the society to their realization. If the resources are largely material, they may be obtained through outputs that take the form of taxation, commands, levees, or expropriations. If they are human, they may result in the organization and mobilization of human groups to ensure their support for the system as a whole as well as for the specific authorities who may be undertaking to adopt and implement the specific goals.

What I am depicting here is, in effect, a vast conversion process. In it the inputs of demands and support are acted upon in such a way that it is possible for the system to persist and to produce outputs meeting the demands of at least some of the members, and retaining the support of most. The system is a way of translating demands and support for a system into authoritative allocations.

The persistence of any type of political system at all can now be redefined. If any stress threatens to destroy the system, its impact will take the form of interfering in some fundamental way with the capacity of the system to keep such a conversion process working. If no outputs related to binding decisions and actions can be provided, the system has broken down. Systems analysis as employed here is not concerned with understanding the operations of specific types of systems, such as a democracy. If it were so used, we could say that such a type of system had failed when it could no longer convert inputs into outputs under the constraints dictated by the nature of the system.

We can now return to stress and cast a somewhat different light on it. What prevents political systems from keeping some kind of conversion process working? At one level the answer is painfully simple. Defeat at the hands of a conqueror, a series of economic crises, or new opportunities arising from exposure to the economy, ideals, and practices of Western culture, as in the case of many traditional African societies, may lead to the permanent destruction of existing systems.

But I have already argued that such an explanation evades the main issues. It describes conditions external or internal to a political system that have been seen to accompany political changes. It does not give us a clue as to how we are systematically to locate and describe the actual processes through which the stresses implied in such events are communicated to a political system.

Through the identification of inputs and outputs as the indicators of more complex combinations of variables, we can now see that it is possible to pinpoint the locus of the stress that may drive the essential variables of a system beyond their critical range. In place of having to weave together all of the varied and threatening disturbances, we are now able to locate the stress by examining what is happening to the input of demands and support. Presumably, under some conditions fluctuations in demands and support will be found to be more stressful on the conversion process than under others. We would then be concerned with knowing something about the typical ways in which, through outputs, a system manages either to abort the occurrence of such conditions, thereby avoiding stress, or to cope with them once they have come about.

Persistence of a system, its capacity to continue the production of authoritative outputs, will depend, therefore, upon keeping a conversion process operating. This conclusion sets a pattern of analysis for us. It suggests that we should examine the following variables: first, the nature of the inputs; second, the variable conditions under which they will constitute a stressful disturbance on the system; third, the environmental and systemic conditions that generate such stressful conditions; fourth, the typical ways in which systems have sought to cope with stress; fifth, the role of information feedback; and finally, sixth, the part that outputs play in these conversion and coping processes. In effect, this outlines a succeeding volume to be devoted to the construction of a substantive theory of political life in systems terms.

THE RESPONSIVE POTENTIAL OF POLITICAL SYSTEMS

It is clear, therefore, that if a systems conceptualization suggests little else, it does present a dynamic model of a political system. As demands and support flow through the system, it is able to get something done. The final product of this activity takes the form of outputs, and these may react back upon what the system may subsequently be called upon to do.

Furthermore, as I have already intimated, this flow is not of a passive sort. It is not analogous to a liquid coursing through a conduit and emerging differently due to an admixture of chemicals en route or to water flowing through a hydroelectric generating plant and performing work in the process. A political system is a goal-setting, self-transforming and creatively adaptive system. It consists of human beings who are capable of anticipating, evaluating, and acting constructively to prevent disturbances in the system's environment. In the light of their goals, they may seek to correct any disturbances that might be expected to occasion stress. The demands and support can be molded to the purposes and desires of members of the system to the extent that knowledge, resources and inclination permit.

Members of the system are not passive transmitters of things taken into the system, digesting them in some sluggish way, and sending them along as outputs that influence other social systems or the political system itself. They are able to regulate, control, direct, modify, and innovate with respect to all aspects and parts of the processes involved. This is what is meant in saying that they are able to cope constructively with stress. It is to theoretical problems raised by a conceptualization such as this, implicit in the idea of a system of behavior, that we must turn if we are to understand how some kind of political life has been able to sustain itself in society.

CONCLUSION

Behavioral research in politics, I suggested at the outset of this volume, means more than the application of the rigorous techniques of science and more than an increased awareness of the canons of scientific inquiry. It represents for the first time a commitment to the broad and essential requirements of scientific knowledge: the search for criteria that within the scientific framework will permit the investigator to test for the relevance of empirical data and at the same time will offer some hope of providing a richer understanding of the phenomena central to his interest. This is uniquely the task of theory and it is to its construction that modern behavioral science has slowly been guiding our footsteps, so slowly indeed that only in the last decade has it become even faintly visible.

To be sure, part of the new, intense excitement in political research revolves around the invention and refinement of novel and rewarding technical tools for the reliable collection, collation, and analysis of data. This could scarcely be otherwise. In political science we have discovered the power that lies in rigorous research at the very time that fascinating technological inventions are being added at a breath-taking pace to the repertoire of all the behavioral sciences. The mechanization of the storage, processing, and retrieval of data has opened up new vistas of inquiry that will prove to be as revolutionary for the social sciences as the discovery of atom-smashing machines for physics or of isotopes for the biological disciplines.[8]

[8] A rapid survey of some of the major efforts in this direction may be obtained from U.S. House of Representatives, Committee on Education and Labor, *Ad Hoc* Subcommittee on a National Research Data Processing and Information Retrieval Center, *Hearings,* 88th Cong., 1st. sess., 1963. See also: *The American Behavioral Scientist,* 6 (1962), an issue devoted to "The New Educational Technology"; P. E. Converse, "A Network of Data Archives for the Behavioral Sciences," *Public Opinion Quarterly,* 28 (1964), 273-86; *Report on the Minnowbrook Conference on Information Retrieval in the Social Sciences* (Syracuse

Political science has moved into the area of rigorous research just in time to be caught up in this new tidal wave of technical innovation with all that it means for the established empirical disciplines in the way of learning new languages, mechanical skills, and even thought processes. Although political science has suffered in its development in the past because of its tardiness in taking advantage of the best that social research had to offer, its very weaknesses have peculiarly enough now turned into a potential source of strength. Unlike the more developed social disciplines, it does not have to suffer the costs of change-over from traditional or antiquated empirical skills, nor does it have to do battle over research concepts in which empirical scholars have developed vested interests. Instead, by virtue of the fact that it is stepping into empirical research with a minimal investment in prior training and empirical concepts, it is free to take full advantage of the opportunities offered by the most advanced of these new mechanized techniques.[9]

At the same time, by virtue of their very potency, the new technical skills have sent forth signals of alarm as though the scientific enterprise had its own built-in regulators. Empirical knowledge is not enough; yet in one sense it threatens to become more than enough. The headlong pace at which empirical data can now be accumulated threatens to inundate the scientific enterprise with an overwhelming and virtually irresistible flood. Some powerful counterforce is required to spare the discipline from being buried under an avalanche of knowledge that can only gain momentum through the decades if it thunders on unchecked. The hyperfactualism of the decades preceding World War II would seem like pure theory compared to the raw data collection and storage now made feasible and actually under way as a result of the startling computer inventions already available.

What we have now is a mere infant's step, a crude beginning in the way of mechanized facilities. New generations of successively more complex computers of almost unimaginable capabilities are already on the horizon. Their invention and perfection will take place at the hands of a new generation of scholars who will be the first to talk machine language from their earliest exposure to arithmetic and mathematics in grade and secondary schools.

---

and Western Reserve Universities, 1961); papers presented to An International Conference on the Use of Quantitative Political, Social and Cultural Data in Cross-National Comparisons at Yale University, 1963; *International Social Science Journal*, 16 (1964), a special issue devoted to "Data in Comparative Research"; a number of articles in *The American Behavioral Scientist*, 7 (1964); and the various issues of *Social Sciences Information* founded in 1962.

[9] This helps us to understand, as a reading of the citations in Footnote 8 would indicate, why political scientists have been providing a major impulse behind the drive in the 1960's for an integrated program for the mechanized storage, processing, and retrieval of social data.

Unlike their predecessors, it is they who will feel entirely at ease with and confident about their relationships to and mastery of the computer. The growth in the introduction and use of such machines for storing and processing information must indeed assume the shape of a steep exponential curve.

If for no other reason than from a strong sense of self-preservation, the scientific enterprise in political research would be compelled to devise a way of controlling and giving meaning to the new and ever-increasing flood of data. It is to theory construction, therefore, that behavioral science in this generation has begun to turn, even if at first slowly and hesitatingly. Through general theory we may hope to give broader meaning and relevance to what might otherwise be essentially increasingly reliable and yet increasingly diverse piecemeal bits of research. For the first time empirically oriented theory has begun to stir the scientific imagination in political research. And as political theorists come to feel more comfortable in the presence of the machines, they too will learn to put the computer to use in the formulation and solution of their own problems with regard to the construction of theory.

In this volume I have not sought to reiterate the persuasive arguments that might be made for the need for such general theory, nor have I attempted to construct such a theory. The one I have already essayed elsewhere,[10] and the other I shall present in a subsequent volume. What I have undertaken here is to demonstrate the kinds of commitments to which we might usefully subscribe if we are to adopt the simple concept "system" in anything but a simplistic way.

For many users to describe political life as a system may just represent a convenient and fashionable substitute for many alternative ways of talking about politics at its theoretically most inclusive level. But if the development of a general political theory arouses our ardor at all, the adoption of system as a concept bears with it certain intellectual commitments. If we wished, we might continue to utilize the concept in a loose and generous way to mean anything that the speaker wished to pour into it. In political research, however, analytic ideas do not grow so luxuriantly that we can afford to be profligate with them. If we are to exploit fully the few ideas that each generation is able to hew out of the hard and recalcitrant rock of nature, we must seek to put them to their most rigorous and, therefore, most powerful theoretical use. In the case of system as a concept, this means that it might be established as the nub of an analytic framework so that around it we could build appropriate secondary concepts into a fullfledged set of interrelated categories. Analysis in terms of systems promises to provide such a conceptual framework; this is its primary justification.

[10] In *The Political System.*

Index

A

Abbott, W. A., 120*fn.*
Acephalous political system, 56
Ackoff, R. L., 24*fn.*
Action frame of reference, 15, 21
Allocation of values, authoritative (*see* Authoritative allocation of values)
Allocative theory, political, 78
Almond, G. A., 1*fn.*, 21*fn.*
American Political Science Association, 5
Analysis as a symbolic system, 27
Analysis of political systems, the level of, 86-90
Analytic system, 37-43 (*see also* System)
Apter, D., 21*fn.*, 89*fn.*
Ashby, W. R., 92*fn.*, 128*fn.*
Authoritative allocation of values,
  as essential variables, 96-97
  identifying criterion of political behavior, 49-50
  meaning, 50
Authorities, 53-54,
  object of support, 116-117
  role in feedback processes, 128-129
  role in generating support, 128-129

B

Bagehot, Walter, 80-81
Bank of England, 60
Barrington, Mrs. R., 82*fn.*
Bassett, R., 60*fn.*
Behaving system, 26
Behavioral approach, 1-22 (*see also* Political behavior),
  as an academic movement, 4-6
  alternative interpretations, 8
  basic tenets, 7
  commitments, nature of, 5-7
  as an intellectual tendency, 6-9
  methodological explanation of, 9-13
  origin of name, 12
  science of politics and, 9
  scientific method and, 17-22
  theory and, 17-22
Behavioral credo, 7
Behavioral sciences,
  origin of name, 12
  theoretical implications, 16
Behavioral theory, 3-4 (*see also* Political theory)
Berelson, B. R., 20*fn.*

137